The Manual for the Early Years SENCO

Second edition

The Manual for the Early Years SENCO

Second edition

Collette Drifte

Los Angeles | London | New Delhi
Singapore | Washington DC

First edition published 2005
Reprinted 2007 (twice)
Second edition published 2010
Reprinted 2013

SAGE Publications Ltd
1 Oliver's Yard
55 City Road
London EC1Y 1SP

SAGE Publications Inc.
2455 Teller Road
Thousand Oaks, California 91320

SAGE Publications India Pvt Ltd
B 1/I 1 Mohan Cooperative Industrial Area
Mathura Road
New Delhi 110 044

SAGE Publications Asia-Pacific Pte Ltd
3 Church Street
#10-04 Samsung Hub
Singapore 049483

Library of Congress Control Number 2009929350

British Library Cataloguing in Publication data

A catalogue record for this book is available from the British Library

ISBN 978-1-84920-157-5
ISBN 978-1-84920-158-2 (pbk)

Typeset by C&M Digitals (P) Ltd, Chennai, India
Printed in Great Britain by Ashford Colour Press Ltd

Contents

Acknowledgements

My thanks always go firstly to the children and practitioners who have taught me so much over the years – they're all very special people.

Thanks, too, go to my editor and friend, Jude Bowen, for her quiet and efficient professionalism and constant support – her faith in me has been an important part of the writing of this book.

And last but not least, thanks to Reinhard, especially for taking over on the days when I had to write and do nothing else!

About the author

Collette Drifte is a freelance author and trainer, with 22 years' experience in mainstream and special education. A former deputy head teacher and now living in Northumberland, she has written numerous articles and books in the fields of early years special needs and early years literacy. She speaks regularly at national conferences and exhibitions, and leads courses, workshops and seminars across the country.

Introduction

Since the first edition of this book was published in 2005, the early years sector has undergone, and indeed is continuing to undergo, major changes in both practice and policy. Further educational and social welfare legislation has been put in place, with, for example, the updated Disability Discrimination Act becoming fully operational. The *SureStart* programme is now a well-established part of early years provision. The Early Years Foundation Stage (EYFS) framework, together with the EYFS Profile and the Common Assessment Framework (CAF), have been implemented and lie at the core of everything practitioners are doing for the children in their care. The career structure and professional development of early years practitioners have been overhauled with, among other things, the introduction of the levels of qualification, and the availability of the Early Years Professional Status (EYPS).

Some of the issues discussed in this book refer to the situation in England, particularly with regards to recent legislation and initiatives. The devolved administrations of Scotland, Wales and Northern Ireland are implementing their own strategies, with their own relevant legislation in place to support these. However, because the fundamentals of best practice are enshrined in all the initiatives, this book is also relevant and appropriate if you are a practitioner in the administrative areas outside England. If you are working in Wales, Scotland or Northern Ireland, therefore, the book will be just as useful and relevant to your working practices.

The book was written initially in response to a request that I've heard many times from newly-appointed Special Educational Needs Coordinators (SENCOs): *I've never done this before – is there a manual or guidebook in Easyspeak that I can get hold of?*

SENCOs are now, by law, appointed to all early years settings and provision. Sadly, many of them will feel they've drawn the short straw, have been thrown in at the deep end and will be totally overwhelmed by the enormity of their responsibilities. They really shouldn't be feeling that way, but if that's how you feel too, then this book is for you! It aims to help and support you, to outline in reader-friendly language exactly what you're supposed to do as your setting's SENCO, and, above all, to enable you to realise you don't have to struggle on your own.

This book shows you how to help and support your colleagues, but also how to access the help and support you may feel you need yourself. It explores your roles and responsibilities as outlined in the *Special Educational Needs (SEN) Code of Practice*, and how these are relevant to the early years sector. Each chapter addresses in detail one of those roles, and the issues behind putting that particular role into practice.

SENCOs work within a huge variety of early years provision, everything from a 'standard' nursery school or class with several practitioners, to a single childminder with a few little ones in their care; from a small village pre-school to a large day nursery offering care from birth to four or five years. Clearly it's impossible to address every type of provision in detail, and therefore some of the advice in this book may need to be adapted to suit your individual needs. However, the book's overall content is there as a framework for you to tweak, adopt, adapt or use as a kick-off (i.e. for you to cherry-pick), to help you formulate practices that will not only make you an efficient SENCO, but, more importantly, will also give you confidence in your role, and help you feel comfortable and happy in it.

I have written this book with the assumption that you are a SENCO completely new to the job and that you're looking for ideas in each area of responsibility in your role. If, however, you're becoming an old(er) hand at the game, you could skip the bits you're conversant with and go to the sections you want to focus on, since each chapter is free-standing, and you won't have to wade through pages of text to get to the core of your question. The format of each chapter is the same: an outline of the key points addressed, a short introduction, the main body of the chapter and the issues it's exploring, followed by a list of relevant CD-ROM resources. There are also copiable resources where appropriate which can be used as they stand, or adapted to your specific setting.

There is a sample SEN policy that you may like to use as a framework for your own, again to be adapted if required, to better suit your particular setting, or to use as it stands. All the forms, policies and samples within the text are on the accompanying CD-ROM. There are useful sample letters to parents/carers that can be used when working together to support a child, and blank referral letters to outside agents, also on the CD-ROM. You can use them as part of your own best practice portfolio, to stimulate discussion with your colleagues, as the basis of in-house professional development sessions, or as part of your overall, wider-ranging policy and practice planning. The CD-ROM also has several PowerPoint presentations which you can use for professional development sessions. These will save you time since they are ready to present, and you can easily print the handouts of the slides. And, of course, you can always tweak them, if you wish, so they become more appropriate to your setting and circumstances.

There are case studies running through the book to highlight specific points where appropriate, all of which feature real children in real situations. To protect the children's identities, their names have been changed. All of the case studies appear in a designated section on the CD-ROM.

There is a Further reading list (page 97) if you would like more information, suggestions and support regarding additional needs. Most of the books recommended have been chosen because they are 'reader-friendly' and also very practical. I have included a few of the more theoretical texts if you wish to study the academic aspects of the subject, such as research findings, but the majority of the titles are not of this genre. If you are following a course of further study you should also refer to your own academic institution's reading list or be guided by your tutor.

There's a section on the CD-ROM showing the Standards that have to be met for the award of Early Years Professional Status. These are clearly closely linked to best practice when it comes to supporting a child with additional needs, and achieving each and every one of the Standards should be the goal of all practitioners, whether or not they register to be officially awarded EYPS. Again, this section will be highly relevant to you, wherever you are (Wales, Scotland and Northern Ireland, as well as England) since the Standards encompass everything that a good early years professional should be doing automatically, and they represent sound goals to aim for in your daily working practices.

Now a few words about terminology. Throughout the book I refer to 'children with special educational needs' or 'children with additional needs', because they are just that: children first and foremost, who happen to have a difficulty, problem or disability. I still hear references to, for example, 'an autistic child' or 'a Down's child', comments which show how deeply entrenched the practice still is of identifying a child by their disability. That disability is (or should be) secondary to the child's right and entitlement to be automatically perceived principally as a child, a human being who happens to have differing needs from the majority of their peers. I refer to 'special educational needs' with reservation, and use the term mainly because it's the common currency within the field, and it's the terminology of the SEN and disability legislation. Some groups representing the world of the disabled (their preferred term) are lobbying to have the phraseology within the legislation altered, but until that happens, we may have to continue using the SEN terminology on many occasions. That doesn't mean, however, that we can't use alternative phrases such as 'differing needs' or 'additional needs' in our everyday dealings. Use the terminology that you and/or the families with whom you're working are comfortable with, but make sure it's not offensive or derogatory.

I'd like to expand a little even on my use of the word 'child'. Clearly, since *Birth to Three Matters* and *Every Child Matters* are enshrined in the EYFS, the child and their welfare from the moment of their birth are of paramount concern to all professionals involved. Therefore while I refer to 'the child' throughout the book, I do in fact mean the baby or the older child, without differentiating.

I use the term 'Individual Education Plans' (IEPs) again with reservation because of the perception that the term may not be appropriate for children in the early years. You may prefer to speak of 'appropriate intervention' or 'effective learning objectives' (I know I do!), but where you see 'IEPs' in the text of this book, please bear in mind the term is being used in its widest sense, and only because it is still current in the legislative SEN jargon. It is equally applicable and relevant to use 'Differentiated Learning Plans', 'Effective Learning Objectives', 'Individual Plans' or 'Play Plans' – whatever is appropriate in your situation and for the child with whom you are working.

Finally, you'll come across the occasional reference to Area SENCOs in the book. At the time of writing, the terms 'Inclusion Consultant', 'Inclusion Officer' or 'Inclusion Adviser' are now being used in some local authorities to refer to Area SENCOs. The terms all apply to designated practitioners performing the same role which, in essence, remains unchanged, regardless of the title of the post held.

Let's consider next what a SENCO needs in order to do the job effectively. Apart from you having to be a sort of early years Houdini, your diplomatic, social, organisational, humanitarian and specialist skills need to be developed, alert and active at any given moment! The Pre-school Learning Alliance (2002) sums up very well what the minimum specifications of a SENCO should be:

Knowledge and understanding

- Diploma in Pre-school Practice or equivalent level 3 qualification
- Knowledge and understanding of the DfES* SEN Code of Practice
- Knowledge of relevant legislation
- Sound understanding of child development, and of children's needs
- Understanding and implementation of equal opportunities

Experience

- Experience of implementing the requirements of the SEN Code of Practice
- 3 years' experience of working in a pre-school setting

(Continued)

(Continued)

- Experience of contributing to the development of Individual Education Plans
- Experience of participating in reviews
- Experience of working with very young children with SEN and their families
- Experience of working in a multi-disciplinary team

Skills

- Sound observation and record-keeping skills
- Ability to plan and implement Individual Education Plans
- Ability to plan and participate in reviews
- Ability to write clear reports
- Ability to work with a range of professionals
- Ability to work with parents and encourage their involvement in their child's learning
- Ability to work in a team and to lead a team of adults

Some specialist pre-schools may demand additional knowledge and expertise in their area of specialist provision. This should also be indicated in the person specification.[1]

Now before you wail in despair and say, *I'm not all those, I can't be all those and I haven't done all those,* have a think about your experience and expertise as a mainstream early years practitioner. You'll have worked closely with parents/carers, colleagues and other professionals. You'll have attended and/or organised meetings, parents' evenings or case conferences. You'll have kept up to date with your records, portfolios, files and profiles. You'll have planned activities, lessons or sessions, adapting and differentiating them to ensure all the children were included. You'll have written reports, recommendations and resumés. By definition, you're an early years practitioner because you have your qualification(s) and knowledge and experience of child development. So, in the final analysis, these specifications of a SENCO aren't a million miles removed from your present situation. If there's an area or two in which you'd like to expand your knowledge and/or experience, ask for the means to do it – if you need it to fulfil your SENCO role effectively, then you should receive it!

One of the most important things to remember is that **you do not have to do everything yourself.** It isn't your job to implement the Individual Education Plans (IEPs), Play Plans or Individual Target Programmes (except where they're for one of 'your' children) or to train your colleagues (unless you have that specific brief because of an extra qualification, for example) or to draw up the SEN policy. You're there as a **coordinator** and as such, you can enable your colleagues to take on board and carry out *their* responsibilities. So don't try to be all things to all people, because you'll end up being of no help to anybody, particularly the children. I hope that this book will enable you to find the ways there are of getting help and support, not only for your colleagues but also for yourself – especially for yourself. If only one or two SENCOs finish this book feeling more confident and with a better belief in themselves, then I'll be a happy author!

Note

1 Pre-school Learning Alliance (2002) *The Role of the Special Educational Needs Co-ordinator in Pre-school Settings.* London: Pre-school Learning Alliance.

* NB the DfES is now the DCSF: the Department for Children, Schools and Families.

1

The SENCO year – a bit of forward planning goes a long way

The **key points** covered in this chapter are:

- Practical strategies for making life as a SENCO both organised and easier.
- Planning the year ahead.
- Statutory assessment – following the timetable.

INTRODUCTION

By taking time to plan an overview of the year ahead, you'll be giving yourself an easy-reference, set-out agenda that will make your life as a SENCO much easier, especially once you're into the busy roll of activities that are woven into the life of an early years setting.

The *Special Educational Needs (SEN) Code of Practice* has an inbuilt timetable for implementing Individual Education Plans (IEPs),* holding reviews (whether of Differentiated Learning Plans [DLPs], IEPs or of Statements of Special Educational Needs) and carrying out statutory assessments. For example, it states that everybody involved in a review must have a fortnight's notice of the review date; they must also have sufficient time to prepare their reports or comments, and to submit or circulate these beforehand.

Keeping up to date with these timed commitments can be difficult and stressful, particularly if your setting has several children whose programmes are operating at different times across the year. Here we'll explore how to plan well ahead of time, enabling you to have a 'glance-at' system that keeps you up to speed.

PRACTICAL STRATEGIES FOR MAKING LIFE AS A SENCO ORGANISED AND EASIER

Assuming you're starting from scratch, it's a good idea first to have a look at your position as SENCO, in the context of your setting. As we discussed in the

(* You may prefer to use 'Effective Learning Outcomes' and/or 'Differentiated Learning Plans'. Whatever method or title you use for these tailor-made plans for the child, their objective remains the same as that of IEPs, which is the term used throughout the *SEN Code of Practice*.)

Introduction, no single book can address the needs of every early years setting, since there's such a variety of provision on offer. However, have a look at the following questions – cherry-pick those that are relevant and appropriate to your situation – and use your answers to focus your thoughts on what you already have and what you might need.

- Are you confident and comfortable in your role as SENCO?

- If not, can you say for what reason(s)?

- Have you received sufficient training?

- Have you received effective training?

- If not, can you access training of the type and standard you require?

- Does your daily/weekly routine enable you to have sufficient dedicated SENCO-time? If not, can you address this?

- Does your setting acknowledge your position as SENCO, e.g. by awarding you recognised status, influence, time, resources, finances, support, etc.?

- Do your setting's resources, equipment, facilities and structure enable you to support children with differing needs effectively?

- Do they enable you to practise inclusion fully and effectively?

- If not, can you address the reasons why not?

- Are you confident in your abilities to support your colleagues and meet their needs in relation to including children with differing needs?

- If not, why not? And what can be done about it?

- Have your colleagues received sufficient and effective training?

- If not, can they access it, or can you access it for them?

- Do you feel supported and valued in your setting by (a) your management team, (b) your colleagues, (c) your Local Authority (LA) or another authority's provision and facilities?

- Do you feel ineffective and/or unable to carry out your role as SENCO? If so, make a list of the reasons why, and decide what can be addressed immediately, and what's short term, medium term and long term.

- Do you have the opportunity to meet with other SENCOs regularly for mutual support, exchange of ideas, sharing of best practice, etc.? If not, can you do something about it?

Keep your answers on file, and revisit them after nine months or so (remember to date your original answers). If you find that you're making progress with your situation, that's fine. If, however, you find that your answers seem to be the same, or haven't changed much, it might be a good idea to review your situation with your management colleagues, highlighting the areas you feel need to be developed. Use the questionnaire above to support your case.

Nuts and bolts (well – maybe a filing cabinet and photocopier/printer/scanner)

Let's have a look now at the down-to-earth stuff. If you're a newly appointed SENCO and wondering where to start, don't despair – just start at the beginning, decide what you need and ask for it!

Here's a starter list:

- *An efficient, confidential and lockable filing system.* Depending on your needs, this could be a filing cabinet with two or three drawers, a small cupboard or even a dedicated drawer within the main, larger filing system. But stake a claim to some SENCO and/or SEN-only space. If you're really lucky, your setting may even give you an area of your own (dare I say *an office?* ...). Some practitioners prefer to keep their records on the computer and print hard copy only when required. If this is the case with you, do make sure that all data are protected or encoded/anonymised to ensure absolute security and confidentiality. This is especially important if you keep records on a shared and/or open computer which can be accessed by personnel who are not authorised to view these files.

- *Folders for the children's records.* Here you should decide as a staff whether to incorporate a section that's designated for their SEN documentation within the child's main folder, or whether you want a separate SEN folder. As a team, decide how you want to file the folders, e.g. by level of the *SEN Code of Practice,* by age group, by setting group, by key worker, in alphabetical order, etc. Don't forget to decide on the type of folder, e.g. ring binders, manila wallets, plastic folders, etc. Your budget will probably help in making this decision!

- *Coloured stickers.* You can use these on the outside of each child's folder, to show at a glance what stage of the *SEN Code of Practice* the child has reached, e.g. a blue sticker for 'Expression of Concern/Differentiated Learning', a green sticker for 'Early Years Action', a yellow sticker for 'Early Years Action Plus' and a red sticker for 'Statutory Assessment'. As the child moves through the different levels, simply put a sticker in the next colour onto the front of the folder.

- *Ring binders and clear plastic insert-wallets.* Use these to file summary sheets, forms, registers, etc. that are currently in use – in other words, the everyday working documents containing information you may want to check frequently and quickly. You might decide as a setting that everybody should have duplicate files with copies of the same information. Make sure that all colleagues keep such files and records in secure and confidential places.

- *Wallets for blank pro forma, record sheets, letters, etc.* Keep these well stocked up – there's nothing more irritating than needing a form or review sheet only to find the wallet is empty. Have a rule that says whoever takes out the last form should make several more copies and leave them in the wallet for future users.

- *A wall calendar with every day on it.* Depending on your setting, you'll need one that shows either the calendar year (January to December) or the academic year (September to August). Keep it displayed so that all staff can see at a glance what's happening in relation to the 'additional needs events', but display it in a confidential place and position.

The paper chase

By definition, you'll probably have a lot of paperwork to store. Much of it will be record forms – blank ones, completed ones, and 'sleeping' ones waiting to be finally discarded – but which ones should you keep? Here's a list:

- Observation forms

- Assessment sheets/baselines/checklists, etc.

- Expression of Concern forms

- Differentiated Learning Plan (DLP) forms (or chosen equivalent)

- Play Plan forms

- Home/setting communication forms or system

- Activity report sheets

- Individual Education Plan (IEP) forms (or their chosen equivalent)

- Review forms

- Summary sheets

- Referral forms (a) to outside agents, (b) for Statutory Assessment

- Educational advice forms – these are usually supplied by the Local Authority (LA)

- Statements of Special Educational Needs

- Letters.

You'll also need to keep in the file your setting's SEN documents and information, and all the documentation from the LA, outside agents, voluntary bodies, etc., that your colleagues may need. *What documentation?* you might ask. The answer is

- your SEN policy (long and short versions, where appropriate)

- the LA's SEN policy and all relevant circulars, directives and documentation issued locally

- Parent Partnership documents

- *SureStart* documents (or their equivalent) relating to additional needs

- contact details of parent support groups, translators, alternative communication agents, etc.

- the *SEN Code of Practice* and the *SEN Toolkit*, plus any other relevant and current government circulars regarding additional needs

- contact details, prospectuses, policies, etc., of outside agents and/or other departments, e.g. social services, health, etc.

- In-service training (INSET) materials and other relevant copiables, documentation, etc. (where relevant).

If you keep the logistical aspects of the job organised and easy to use, life as a SENCO will be less fraught. It *is* a demanding job, and you don't need the added stress of trying to find records, contact details, local procedures, etc. which have been lost and are now in a heap of damp documents piled up on a work surface in the Water Play area!

Planning the year ahead

It will depend on your setting what you will need to plan and how. For example, if you're a SENCO in a large primary school, you'll have more manpower, time and resources than if you're SENCO in a pre-school or for a group of childminders. You'll need to assess what you have to hand and how you can exploit it, in order to do the job effectively. There's no doubt that the role of SENCO involves plenty of paperwork, so getting this under control must be one of your priorities. If you and your computer have a close relationship, use a good spreadsheet program to plan the year ahead. Setting up the calendar at the beginning may involve a bit of a time-investment on your part, but once the job's done, all you'll need to do in future years is tweak the fine details.

Divide your jobs into less frequent ones (the annual or biannual happenings) and frequent ones (the ongoing daily, weekly or monthly stints, or those that happen every three months/each term) and decide which are happening when. Decide, too, which dates are non-negotiable and log these onto the calendar before you do anything else. Let's have a look at this in more detail.

Less frequent jobs

First of all, identify the whole-setting jobs and commitments that take place across the year. Here's a list, although some of the items on it may not apply to you, depending on your setting:

- whole-setting assessment sessions, e.g. medical and/or dental checks, baseline/checklist assessments for mass admissions, etc.

- INSET sessions (your own and/or your colleagues') and the dates these are scheduled

- annual reviews of Statements of Special Educational Needs, and biannual reviews where relevant

- annual and/or three-monthly/termly commitments involving the children, e.g. trips, outings, visits, the photographer, pantomimes and other social events, etc.

- times where you can expect large numbers of children to be absent, e.g. high season holiday periods, etc.

Log onto your calendar any dates that you know are definite, even if those booked for much later in the year may need to be rescheduled or cancelled. This will help you to avoid double booking. By keeping the year planner near the telephone, you can see at a glance whether a suggested date made by a caller is convenient.

Frequent jobs

Next, identify the events that happen every three months (or every term), every month or every week. Among these might be:

- your own regular meetings, e.g. a staff meeting every Thursday afternoon, a meeting with other SENCOs on the third Wednesday of the month, Parent/Staff Group meetings every fourth Monday afternoon, etc.

- regular and/or arranged visits by outside agents, e.g. the health visitor calls in every other Monday, the educational psychologist comes on the first Tuesday after each half-term holiday, the social worker pops in every Thursday afternoon, etc.

- reviews of DLPs, Play Plans, IEPs, etc., whether these are every six weeks or every three months, as appropriate

- meetings to review the setting's SEN policy

- meetings with the governors (if appropriate to you)

- parents'/carers' open days or evenings (if appropriate).

Again, log these onto the year planner and once they're in place, you can play around with the free dates for other meetings or reviews and so on, that will crop up as the year rolls along. It's a good idea first to get into the habit thing every Monday of checking the week's bookings, commitments and jobs on the 'To Do' list.

Also check:

- the review schedule for the fourth week from where you are, and log in all the 'To Dos' for each review, on the relevant date. (For a more detailed discussion of these 'To Dos', see the section *IEP reviews* in Chapter 4, page 41)

- this week's IEP listings to see who's been on what level and for how long

- whether there are any meetings to arrange regarding these IEPs

- whether any outside agents are due to make support visits.

By now, your year planner will be starting to fill up quite a bit, and you'll also be beginning to see why it's a good idea to have an overview of what's happening on your additional needs agenda.

Once you've filled in the immoveable feasts on your year planner, you'll need to update it on at least a weekly basis. If you can, get into the habit of checking each evening whether you have marked something up that was arranged during the day.

MON	TUES	WED	THURS	FRI	SAT	SUN
	1	2 David Jones's docs all in yet?	3 3.30: Policy review – whole staff	4	5	6
7 Suzie Scott's docs all in yet? 3.30: SENCO meeting	8	9 Biscuits etc. for David's review?	10 Send invites & docs for Suzie Scott's review (24th)	11 10.00: David Jones's IEP review	12	13
14 Ask for docs for Sam Brown's review (due 10.04.)	15	16 Vikki B's IEP 3 wks old – check progress	17	18 10.00: Ed. Psych. re: John F. (Mum coming)	19	20
21	22	23 Biscuits etc. for Suzie's review?	24 10.00: Suize Scott's IEP review	25	26	27
28 9.00 – 3.30 Staff SEN training day	29	30 Mrs Smith's group on farm visit	31 pm: Charity Santa Dash	1 Ask for docs for Gita Rani's review (due 28.05)		

Figure 1.1 An example of a completed month from a year planner form

It's so easy in the hubbub of a busy early years setting to come off the phone and be so distracted by one of the children marmelising another, that you forget to make a note in your diary of an arranged visit or review meeting or whatever. Taking a few minutes of peace and quiet at the end of the day will help keep you up to date, and may even save you some embarrassment later when everybody turns up for a review meeting that you'd completely forgotten about!

STATUTORY ASSESSMENT – FOLLOWING THE TIMETABLE

Because the *SEN Code of Practice* gives a specific timetable for Statutory Assessments and the issuing of Statements of Special Educational Needs, you might find it a good idea to have a separate calendar or diary dedicated to this level of the process. On a routine year planner the day spaces can look quite busy and crowded over time and you may miss an important date in the schedule of a Statutory Assessment. Having a dedicated planner will avoid this. Again, a computer spreadsheet or even a simple wall-hanging calendar will do nicely.

Once you have a child going down the Statutory Assessment route, mark on the calendar the dates showing what should be happening and when. You can work these out by looking at the flow chart on page 120 of the *SEN Code of Practice* and calculating the appropriate dates following the date that your child's referral was received by the LA. You can also check this by ringing them to confirm the receipt and the relevant date. So, for example, if your child's referral was received by the LA on 3 March, the obligatory timetable is this:

	3 March	LA receives referral
by	14 April	LA must decide whether to assess (i.e. within 6 weeks)
by	23 June	LA asks for and receives advice, and must decide whether to make a Statement of Special Educational Needs (i.e. over the next 10 weeks, which is 16 weeks from receipt of referral)
by	7 July	LA must issue either draft Statement or reasons for not making a Statement (i.e. within the next 2 weeks, which is 18 weeks from receipt of referral)
by	1 September	LA must issue final Statement (i.e. within the next 8 weeks, which is 26 weeks from receipt of referral)

Figure 1.2

The dates on your wall calendar could therefore look something like this:

3 March	LA received Jade Kirby's referral (confirmed on phone 8 March – spoke to Kelly Blythe, SEN Dept.)
14 April	Has LA decided whether to assess Jade Kirby? If not, chase.
28 April	Has LA requested educational advice re: Jade Kirby yet? If not, chase.
23 June	Has LA received advice re: Jade Kirby? Has it decided whether to make Statement? If not yet notified, chase.
7 July	Has LA issued draft Statement or reasons for not making a Statement for Jade Kirby? If not, chase.
1 September	Has LA issued Jade Kirby's final Statement? If not, chase.

Figure 1.3

Once the child's Statement of Special Educational Needs has been issued, there'll be a strict timetable of reviews. Usually the LA convenes these reviews so, while as SENCO you organise in-house review meetings, you're unlikely to be expected to do the Annual or Biannual reviews. However, you'll still need to collate the paperwork, educational advice and feedback from all the involved agents within the setting.

Above all, you must continue to make sure the child's parents/carers are being kept informed, advised of their rights and consulted for their opinion, as indeed so must the child, where possible and appropriate. They may need extra support during this time, so it's important you check whether they're comfortable with the process and understand fully what's happening. And, of course, it goes without saying that the child must continue to receive support and help too.

The legislation requires an Annual Review to be held on the anniversary of the issue of the Statement. For very young children, an interim review will also be held (i.e. every six months), although this will be on a less formal level. Because the needs and development of children in the early years stage can change rapidly and fundamentally, their progress must be monitored very closely and reviewed more often than older children's.

From the content of this chapter, you can see it's not hugely demanding to put together an organised and smoothly-run schedule. As with all things, time and effort invested in the beginning will pay dividends in the end. Once you have a system in place that you're comfortable with, and that you find easy to run, much of the paper-chasing that the SENCO's role demands will be manageable. Don't become frustrated if you haven't got it all in place within 24 hours. Take time to let your system 'bed down', so you can see how and where it works for you, and where it's causing you headaches; give it two or three months/one term and then look at it again to see how you can change it to suit your needs.

Remember, you're not on your own. If you're unsure about anything, do ask your Inclusion Consultant. They may also be stumped by your query, but they'll know where to go to get it sorted out!

2

Policy and practice – the unbroken circle

The **key point**s covered in this chapter are:

- The policy/practice issue – which comes first?
- The difference between inclusion and integration.
- Policies as working documents, constantly under review.
- The role of the SENCO in policy development and implementation.
- What needs to go into an inclusive special educational needs (SEN)/Inclusion policy?
- The legal implications and obligations of the Disability Discrimination Act 1995.
- Planning and implementing an inclusive SEN policy – some practical ideas.

INTRODUCTION

Here we'll be exploring an overview of SEN policy issues. If you're new to the concept, this chapter should answer your queries, worries and questions about 'how it's done'. As the *Code of Practice* stipulates that all settings should have an SEN policy, it's likely that there's already one in place in your setting, and you won't be starting from scratch. The sections on reviewing the policy will be more appropriate if you're in this situation. However, if you are indeed starting from nothing, perhaps because you're in a newly-established setting or a newly-organised early years provision, the chapter as a whole will help. The main thing to remember is that creating a policy isn't rocket science, and by the end of the chapter I hope you'll feel confident enough in helping your setting to write and continue to review a good, inclusive policy.

THE POLICY/PRACTICE ISSUE – WHICH COMES FIRST?

The *SEN Code of Practice* states that all early years settings receiving government funding must write and put into practice an SEN policy. But aside from the legal requirement, writing such a policy is an excellent way for you to review your practices and philosophy, and to focus on inclusion. For this reason, private and non-maintained settings will also need to write and implement their own SEN policies.

If you're due to be inspected by Ofsted you may well feel pressurised into writing the policy so it's to hand if necessary. It's important not to give in to this pressure, since

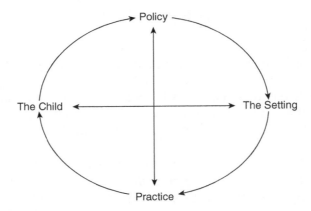

Figure 2.1   The policy/practice issue – an unbroken circle

you could end up with a poorly-planned policy that does everything but ensure the children's entitlements. If you're in the early stages of the process, note in your action plan document your intention to formulate your SEN policy in the short to medium term, or, if you've actually started, show in the action plan what stage you've reached. Give yourself and any colleagues the time to do the job properly which, in the long run, will ensure you 'do' inclusion well.

If you're starting to write your first SEN policy, you may be wondering whether you should write the policy and then use it in your working practices, or work out which practices suit your children and the setting best, and then write the policy. The reality is that this concept of policy/practice is actually an unbroken circle – your good practice should influence your policy, and your policy should enable this good practice to continue and develop.

Don't re-invent your setting's wheel. Look at what you're doing now with regard to the children who have additional needs. You're almost certainly differentiating their work and activities; you'll have allocated a key worker to them; you'll be keeping careful records and continually monitoring their progress; you'll have a good system of communication with their parents/carers and you'll be thinking 'Where next?' It's a safe bet that much of what goes into an SEN policy is already happening in your daily routine. When you read the section below, *What needs to go into an inclusive SEN policy?*, try to establish which things you're already doing. You'll probably be pleasantly surprised to find that in fact you're well on the way to having the framework of your policy already done. So let the policy lead the practice and the practice lead the policy – and don't lose sleep over the process!

THE DIFFERENCE BETWEEN INCLUSION AND INTEGRATION

Inclusion is now automatically part of the planning in early years settings, but you may still hear people referring to 'integration'. The two terms are often used interchangeably but they do not mean the same thing. 'Integration' was the buzzword after the SEN legislation of 1981, when mainstream schools began integrating children with special needs, into their settings. Over time, though, there's been a gradual change in how we can best support children with additional needs, and the concept of inclusion has developed from this, with the term itself coming into more regular use from about 1996.

So what is the difference between inclusion and integration? Let's have a look.

- *Integration* means having children with additional needs in a mainstream setting and expecting them to change in order to 'fit in'. Their disability or difficulty is seen as coming from within and needing to be 'cured' or corrected by remedial means. Integration doesn't encourage or make possible any changes in the setting, whether of attitudes or practices by its staff, to enable children to join in all activities as fully as possible. In other words, *the onus is on the child to change.* This is known as the medical model of the child and their difficulties.

- *Inclusion* means having children with additional needs in a mainstream setting and making sure the setting's attitudes, policies and practices change and adapt so that each child can join in as fully as possible. In other words, *the onus is on the setting and everybody involved in it to change, if necessary.* The child's disabilities or difficulties are seen as part of the whole picture. This is known as the social model of the child and their difficulties.

This represents an important distinction and as the SENCO for your setting or cluster you're in a superb position to spread the word and make sure that everybody understands the difference between the two concepts and uses the correct terminology.

POLICIES AS WORKING DOCUMENTS, CONSTANTLY UNDER REVIEW

As we've seen, your policy should most definitely not be a document quickly downloaded from computer software, ready for next week's Ofsted inspection and then dumped in the back of a filing cabinet. It's your key to including all children in your setting and it's also a framework on which to develop your SEN provision. In other words, it's a working document produced by your setting to let everybody know what your aims are with regard to the children in your care. It should be constantly changing and being adapted to suit your needs at any particular point in time, and continuously being challenged, questioned and analysed for its effectiveness. It isn't a 'one-size-fits-all' document, written and then put aside, but a well-used reference for developing and recording the good practice that goes on in your setting. So keep tweaking it to make it work!

THE ROLE OF THE SENCO IN POLICY DEVELOPMENT AND IMPLEMENTATION

Maybe you've never written a policy before and you're feeling panic at the very thought of it. If you are, but as the SENCO you can't avoid the issue, take heart – no one in your setting can run away from it, or dump it all on you, because policy-making has to be a joint effort. The important thing is not to see this as an awesome task, an obligation, a useless exercise, or just something to keep the Ofsted inspector happy. A carefully planned, well-written SEN policy will, in the long run, save you a great deal of time and it will also ensure that the little ones in your care receive the support and the enjoyable experience of early years education that they're entitled to.

Your role is to oversee the day-to-day operation of the policy, and just how you can go about this will be explored in the relevant chapters of this book. But if you're starting from scratch, your main task is to organise the practicalities of getting people together to do the planning, discussing and writing up. Once again, there's more about how to do this later. Remember – you're not on your own and you can get help, support and advice from various people.

As we saw earlier, it's likely that writing your SEN policy is going to be a question of recording the things you're already doing. While you, as SENCO, will see to the daily operation of the policy, it is, in fact, a total ownership thing – everybody should make sure it's being acted on wherever they can. It's only by actually working with the policy that its strengths and weaknesses will be highlighted, so all 'chalk-face workers' must continually think about where the policy works well and where it's becoming a pain, for whatever reason. It's important you encourage them to tell you what they have discovered, for discussion at the next policy review.

WHAT NEEDS TO GO INTO AN INCLUSIVE SEN POLICY?

The *SEN Code of Practice* suggests what you need to include and among the most important are the following:

- *Information about the aims and objectives of the policy.* Ask yourselves, 'What are our aims in the policy we're drawing up?' 'Are we aiming for the inclusion of children with different needs?' 'Does our policy make sure that happens?'

- *The name of the SENCO and any specialities offered by members of staff.* Give the name of any practitioner within the setting who has a qualification and/or training in any field of SEN, and what their speciality is. For example, 'Our Manager, Anne Jones, holds an MEd, and has specialised in working with children who have autism'.

- *The arrangements for provision for children who have special educational needs.* Ask yourselves, 'How are we going to support children with different needs in terms of resources, staffing, time and so on?' Look at how the setting is organised, run, staffed and equipped, reviewing these and making sure each element includes children with additional needs, adapting it if necessary. Keep this as general as possible because you can't possibly plan for every kind of additional need or condition. Such 'tailor-made' provision will come when you're admitting a child with an identified difficulty and you have to plan their Inclusion Programme or Individual Education Plan (IEP).

- *The arrangements for admission of children with special educational needs.* Agree on your approach to admitting children with additional needs; for example, whether you'll have a transition or familiarisation period, whether you'll invite parents/carers to stay with the child initially, whether it will be necessary to make some adaptations within the setting, and so on.

- *The arrangements for identifying and assessing special educational needs.* The yardstick that you will use for identification and assessment must be outlined in the policy. Ask yourselves, 'Who will do it? When? Where? How?' For example, will it be done by the child's own key practitioner, the SENCO, the manager/head? Will it be done at a set time, or at a time when the assessor happens to be 'free' to do it? Will it be done within your normal daily activity sessions or as a designated assessment/observation session? What form will it take: will you use the Early Years Foundation Stage profile (or the equivalent system for your area), standardised assessments, observations (and what type of observation?) and so on?

- *The arrangements for providing access for children with special educational needs to a balanced and broadly based curriculum.* Ask yourselves how you'll ensure that all the children, regardless of their ability or the difficulties being experienced, will have the opportunities and experiences of the full curriculum on offer, whether this is the Early Years Foundation Stage, the National Curriculum, or another equivalent curriculum for your area. Review your resources and how you use them, whether the equipment, games and activities can be effectively and appropriately used by children with differing needs. It may mean adjusting the timetable, the venue, the staffing, etc., to enable the children with additional needs to access everything that's on offer. Review how you plan and implement DLPs/Play Plans/IEPs, making sure that your procedures can actually result in effective support for each child.

- *The procedures for reviewing the needs of a child with special educational needs.* When, where and how will reviews be carried out? Who will be involved? *The SEN Code of Practice* does offer suggestions, but some things are unique to each setting. Because you have to consider your own facilities – timetable, staffing, clientèle, and so on – in the decision-making, your agreed arrangements will be unique.

- *The partnership with parents/carers and other establishments or agencies.* This includes parents'/carers' access to Parent Partnership Services (PPS) and/or Independent Parental Support Services (IPSSs). Do you have procedures in place for making sure parents/carers are made aware of their rights? Do you have arrangements up and running for parents/carers who don't speak English or who have alternative communication systems themselves, such as sign language? Examine your links with other establishments such as schools, childminding networks and other early years settings – who are these with and how are they maintained? Ask yourselves, too, whether the links help with the inclusion of all children. And don't forget links with other outside agencies such as social services, health, education welfare services, child protection agencies and voluntary organisations. How are your links with these maintained? Look at your arrangements for staff training in the area of SEN and Inclusion – how will you ensure that staff can access this? Your local *SureStart* scheme, and Local Authority (LA) will offer this either in terms of in-house training, or as information and advice about accessing training offered by other providers. It's up to you as SENCO to make sure you can all tap this source when you need to.

- *The criteria for evaluating the success of the SEN policy.* Ask yourselves when and how the policy will be reviewed, how everybody will decide its strengths and weaknesses, and how you'll make any required changes. As the policy is used on a daily basis its weaknesses will soon become apparent, and how serious these are and how quickly they need to be addressed. Again, there isn't a blueprint for this because each setting is unique.

Some professionals would advocate that a policy (any policy) should not be any longer than one side of A4 paper. It's debatable whether any of those professionals have actually tried doing this, unless they have used 8-point font and single spacing, written both horizontally and vertically on both sides of the page! However, if you feel that your policy is turning out to be a bit on the long side, you can shorten it. Leave out the fine details that are in the main policy and offer a condensed version for anybody who'd prefer one. If the full version is requested and/or needed, you can then issue or use it as appropriate. The full version would be made available to Ofsted inspectors or perhaps any parents/ carers who are going to be involved in individualised planning for their child who has additional needs, while the condensed version can be made available to those people who don't, at that point, want the full text. As long as you make sure everybody knows that the complete version is available whenever they want it, you will have met the needs of all concerned. Don't forget to consider whether you will need copies of the policy translated into other languages. If you do, make sure that the translation is of a high standard and accurate. You'll find examples of both a shortened and a full-length SEN policy on the CD-ROM.

THE LEGAL IMPLICATIONS AND OBLIGATIONS OF THE DISABILITY DISCRIMINATION ACT 1995

When you and your colleagues plan your policy, and put it into practice, you may find the following information useful, because you have a legal obligation to implement the Disability Discrimination Act 1995 (DDA). Since September 2002, the Act has embraced *all* providers of early years services. In other words, no matter what your setting, provision or establishment, if you have the care and education of children as your responsibility, you must fulfil the requirements of the DDA.

Under the DDA, the definition of disability is 'a physical or mental impairment which has a substantial or long-term adverse effect on (a person's) ability to carry out normal day-to-day activities'. Be careful of this definition, though, because a child can have a disability but may not necessarily have additional needs. For example, a child with a visual difficulty may be deemed to have a disability but, because they have appropriate spectacles and desk-lighting equipment, they aren't likely to be classed as having additional needs because their educational progress is probably unimpeded.

Under the DDA, you have two main obligations to fulfil. You must:

- not treat a disabled child 'less favourably' than others in the setting

- make 'reasonable adjustments' to ensure disabled children are fully included.

(The 'reasonable adjustments' refer here to removing physical barriers to learning so, as we discuss in Chapter 3, under the Act, you have an 'anticipatory duty', and need to be prepared. As soon as your planning and budget will allow, you should make appropriate adjustments to your building. Remember, you cannot wait for a child with a particular disability to be admitted before you make the relevant changes to your setting.)

You can see, therefore, how highly relevant the DDA is to you and your colleagues when planning the Inclusive policy, and, arguably more importantly, when you are implementing that policy.

For more very useful information on implementing the DDA efficiently, see *Early Years and the Disability Discrimination Act 1995: What Service Providers Need to Know*. Details of how you can obtain this must-have booklet are in the Further reading section on page 97.

PLANNING AND IMPLEMENTING AN INCLUSIVE SEN POLICY – SOME PRACTICAL IDEAS

The *SEN Code of Practice* requires that everybody involved with your setting must write an inclusive SEN policy **together** in order to publish it and make it available to anyone who's interested. As we have seen, you should plan and write this policy with the concept of inclusion running through it. Here's a summary of how the policy itself is actually everybody's baby:

- Its *management* is the manager's or head's responsibility.

- *Its planning, writing and publishing* are done by all persons appropriately involved with your setting.

- Its day-to-day *operation* is your responsibility, as the SENCO.

- Its *implementation* is the responsibility of you and all your colleagues within their own areas.

So where on earth do I start? you might be asking. Never fear – once again, the answer lies in the planning and in giving both yourself and your colleagues time to do the job properly. As with all things, good groundwork is vital. It may be useful before you tackle the policy-writing to conduct an Inclusive Practice Audit, together with your colleagues, to establish where your setting is in this regard. Many SENCOs are now undertaking these to provide an information base from which to support the development of both good practice and a sound Inclusion policy. The audit should seek to answer three fundamental questions:

1. Does the setting offer fair and equal opportunities to *all* the children?

2. Does the setting recognise and then attempt to overcome any barriers to learning that may be present?

3. Does the ethos of the setting embrace inclusion in its fullest sense, and therefore does the setting practice inclusion fully?

There are several good Audits available commercially, but before you spend precious funds, check whether your Area SENCO/Inclusion Adviser and/or your LA have developed a home-grown Inclusion Audit. Once you and your colleagues have carried out the audit, you'll be in a sound position to move forward with developing your policy.

Like Rome, a good policy isn't created in a day! Realistically, you'll need several meetings to agree on it and write it, and it'll be at least eight or nine months after you've put it into practice (or put your practices down on paper – which comes first?) and given it a good few tweaks and revisions before you will begin to see its strengths and weaknesses.

However, let's assume you haven't yet done anything about your SEN policy. Here are some suggestions to get the process started:

- Arrange a meeting of everybody involved in your setting, including parents/ carers and, if required, any outside agencies who could make a useful contribution to the discussion. (You can get the children's opinions during contact time.) As the SENCO, you're the person most likely to be in touch with everybody who should be involved.

- Before the meeting, circulate copies of any LA or setting management documentation that's relevant to SEN and Inclusion policies. This helps to focus people's minds and gives them a chance to note down anything they want to ask, comment on or discuss.

- If you can, designate a Chair and one other person to take the Minutes – don't do both of these yourself, as you need to be on the ball for making suggestions and answering queries. The Chair should be someone who can keep the discussion focused and guided.

- Work through each section of the proposed policy, discussing it thoroughly. You're unlikely to crack this in a single meeting, so be prepared for another couple of sessions before you're all happy with the draft.

- Ask for a volunteer to write the draft document, unless you have time to do it yourself.

- Before finishing the meeting, book the date of the next one while you have everyone captured! Diaries become full very quickly, so make the next date immediately.

- Include everything in the draft that was agreed at the meeting(s). Make sure each person involved has a copy of it shortly before the next meeting. This will help refresh people's memories and will give them a chance to prepare their questions and queries, saving time in the meeting itself.

- Hold a meeting to finalise and approve the policy document. Agree on how you'll get the policy to the parents/carers and other interested parties. You may also need to consider whether you need a translated version for people who don't speak English or who have alternative communication systems, and how you'll get the document to people who don't or can't come to the setting very often.

- Agree a start-date for the policy and book its first review meeting in about a term or three months, so it has a chance to pan out and you can see how it's beginning to work in practice.

- At the policy review meeting, especially if this is the first SEN policy that you've written, be prepared to make changes. Don't be afraid to do this. A policy is a working document and only by using it in practice will its strengths and weaknesses be highlighted. There'll be some things you want to change, but also some other things that are so good you'll want them to remain.

- Agree any changes and issue the revised policy to everybody as soon as possible, then get the revised policy into practice immediately and keep monitoring the changes to make sure that they're doing what you wanted them to do. When something occurs to you about the policy, jot down a note or two as soon as you can, then later you'll have a memory-jogger to hand when you and your colleagues discuss any changes to be made.

- If you would prefer to use a different terminology from 'special educational needs', you could use phrases such as 'differing needs', 'different needs' or 'additional needs'. Whichever phraseology you choose is, of course, a matter of personal choice for your setting and its circumstances, but above all, for the children in your care and their parents/carers.

 CD-ROM Resources for this chapter

An example of an Inclusive SEN Policy (short version)

An example of an Early Years Inclusive SEN Policy (full-length version)

Supporting colleagues – giving help where it's needed

The **key points** covered in this chapter are:

- Support for the SENCO.
- The role of the SENCO in supporting colleagues.
- Practical ways of supporting colleagues.
- Delivering in-service special educational needs (SEN)/Inclusion training.

INTRODUCTION

If you're a new SENCO, you're possibly feeling a bit overwhelmed and unsure of what to do. This chapter explores some of the issues that may arise when you are supporting your colleagues and considering how you can best tackle this aspect of the role. The most important thing to remember is that *you don't have to do it all yourself,* and you must let everybody know this. It's also important that you find out where to go for support for yourself, since you must have this in order to support your colleagues effectively. The people of the north east of England have a lovely saying that sums it all up:

> *Shy bairns get nowt.*

There's plenty of help around, so find out where it is, and ask for it!

SUPPORT FOR THE SENCO

If you haven't looked at the self-posed questions in Chapter 1 (see page 6), now might be a good time to go back and have a little ponder. It's vital that you're comfortable and confident in your role as SENCO, since an unhappy professional won't be anywhere near as effective as one who's clear about their way forward. Before you're in a strong position to support your colleagues, you'll need to ensure your own needs and requirements are met. Examine your level of knowledge and expertise, and/or confidence in the field of additional needs. Ask yourself whether you're able to demonstrate to colleagues your:

- commitment to and good practice of inclusion

- awareness that you, and all your colleagues, have a duty and responsibility to identify children with potential additional needs

- ability to identify children's additional needs and plan effective ways to support them

- management and organisation of resources, personnel and time (your own as well as others')

- knowledge of effective teaching strategies and techniques

- knowledge of and familiarity with the Early Support Materials which are part of the EYFS, or familiarity with the relevant curricular requirements and materials for your area

- knowledge of the EYFS, or equivalent curriculum, and its sections relevant to supporting children with additional needs

- ability to analyse and exploit children's learning styles

- knowledge of SEN legislation, recent research and information

- leadership and decision-making abilities

- communication and cooperative skills.

You may well be able to think of other areas not on this list that you'd like to develop or refine. When you've identified your needs, liaise with your manager or head to explore ways of fulfilling them.

During this process, it's easy to lose confidence in yourself and begin to believe you can't do the job. Try not to fall into this trap, because you *can* do the job. Here are a few fundamentals to remember.

It's vitally important that you:

- recognise and feel confident about your expertise, experience and abilities – you wouldn't be in the job if you weren't capable of doing it

- don't feel de-skilled because of an impression that you have to be all things to all people – it's a false impression, and de-skilled is the last thing you are

- recognise and accept your limitations, however, and then do something about it – nobody will think less of you for asking for help; quite the reverse

- link up with any SENCO group or network that meets in your locality – this will give you a source of ideas, help and support, information, and somewhere to find out what's available that may be useful

- let your manager or head know of anything happening within your setting that you're uneasy about – children with additional needs are the most vulnerable little ones in your care, and if any element in the setting adds to that vulnerability, you must act to stop it

- remember that your colleagues should support you, as well as the other way around – they can make helping a child much more effective by playing their part to the full, including giving you support too, so ask for it.

If you're working from a non-school setting (e.g. kindergarten, pre-school, child-minding network, or *SureStart*, etc.) always have your Area SENCO's/Inclusion Consultant's phone number near to hand, as they're almost sure to be your first point of contact for help. Even if they can't provide it personally, they'll be able to point you in the right direction. Link up with your local primary schools which can give you another strand of resources, help and support.

The *SEN Code of Practice* acknowledges that to do the job effectively, the SENCO needs to have time allocated for SEN work, and suggests that the SENCO should be a member of the senior management team. This may be difficult to achieve in a non-maintained setting or a widely-scattered situation such as a childminding network or a large rural area. If you're finding time a problem, discuss the situation with your line manager and point out what the difficulties are. Explore ways of addressing the problem, e.g. delegating some of the paperwork, reducing your other commitments, allocating some non-contact time, etc. Time management and paperwork are recognised difficulties within the job, and you must exploit every opportunity to address these.

THE ROLE OF THE SENCO IN SUPPORTING COLLEAGUES

The *SEN Code of Practice* states that part of the SENCO's role is to advise and support the other practitioners in the setting. Defining how to do this would be a bit like asking how long a piece of string is. The quality, type, and quantity of support depend very much on each setting's situation, and even then all this will change from year to year.

If you're starting out to assess what your colleagues' needs are, your first course of action should be to ask them. Your perception of what they need (and/or want) may be very different from theirs. Again, how you go about this will depend on your setting. Maybe you can draw up a list of needs during a conversation over a cup of coffee with your colleagues, or maybe you rarely have the chance for such an informal get-together so will need a different way of gathering the information, e.g. distributing a questionnaire.

However you glean your answers, the following suggestions may help to focus thoughts (your own and/or your colleagues') when assessing professional needs within your setting.

Consider whether any colleague needs help to:

- understand the concept of inclusion (not integration) and how to practise it

- identify children with additional needs

- appropriately assess children with additional needs

- take part in planning differentiated work and activities for the child

- formulate Individual Education Plans (IEPs), Differentiated Learning Plans (DLPs) or Play Plans

- monitor the effectiveness of the IEPs/DLPs and adjust them if appropriate

- devise effective strategies and techniques for working with children who have difficulties with their

  - communication and interaction

  - cognition and learning

  - behavioural, emotional and social development

  - sensory and/or physical development

- prepare for and take part in IEP reviews

- understand the processes behind Early Years Action, Early Years Action Plus and Statutory Assessment

- work with the child's parents/carers

- work with outside agencies

- work with colleagues within the setting.

Once you have your feedback, discuss with your manager or head ways of addressing the issues raised by your colleagues.

PRACTICAL WAYS OF SUPPORTING COLLEAGUES

Let's look at some strategies for offering support to your colleagues. You may need to peel back the institutional layers and review your setting from the bottom up (or even the top down!) to see where it supports the staff, and therefore offers effective support for the children.

The curriculum/educational opportunities

Have a look at the curriculum you're offering, whether this is under the banner of standardised curricula (Early Years Foundation Stage, National Curriculum, or another curriculum implemented in your area) or from a particular philosophy or practice (for example, Reggio Emilio, Feuerstein or Montessori), and decide whether it's truly inclusive. Children with additional needs will be effectively supported within your setting only if your curriculum:

- is regularly reviewed

- is well planned

- is well organised

- facilitates the learning styles and needs of the children

- accommodates the teaching styles and all-round skills of the practitioners

- is constantly evaluated and monitored

- is adjusted where it fails to address the needs of the children.

When, as a staff, you're planning work, sessions, activities, etc., these curriculum characteristics may help you to focus on the curriculum and ask yourselves, *Is this working?*

Support within the working areas

You should explore the type, extent and level of support for practitioners within the working areas – at the chalk face, so to speak. There are many ways of providing this, again depending on your particular situation and the specific needs of any given child. These can include:

- differentiated Learning Plans, Effective Learning Objectives, Individual Education Plans or Statements of Special Educational Needs – the roadmaps towards enabling the child to develop and progress

- specific teaching and/or management techniques

- an allocated Learning Support Assistant (LSA) or Teaching Assistant (TA)

- support from an outside agent working with the child and/or the key practitioner

- time allocated for working with the child, either on a one-to-one basis or within a group (i.e. the rest of the children are handed over to another practitioner)

- adapted resources and/or furniture

- specialised equipment.

Discussing these issues with the key worker will enable you to decide together what is the most effective method of supporting them. By encouraging your colleague to share their requirements with you, you'll be better placed to ensure they receive the help they feel they need.

Outside links

You can access support for yourself and/or your colleagues by developing and maintaining links with a number of organisations or bodies outside your setting. Doing this will give you an opening for:

- information

- people

- services.

All of these can offer support in a variety of ways.

If you're in a non-school setting, establish links with your local primary/first/ infant/nursery school, and make sure you maintain those links; suggest regular meetings or get-togethers; ask whether their SENCO would be willing to share ideas and expertise with you on a two-way basis; invite their staff to the occasional social 'do'; offer to share your early years resources or equipment or facilities, etc. Setting up such links and sharing best practice can ensure a standardised and seamless provision for all the children in your area, as well as providing a source of support and help for the practitioners involved.

Make sure your colleagues know that this support and advice is available from your local authority support services. What they will offer you depends on the need you identify within the setting. There's a fuller discussion of this in Chapter 7, which explores the services and their role.

Always remember that your Area SENCO/Inclusion Consultant is there as the first port of call, as are your *SureStart* team. If they can't provide the support you need directly, they'll certainly know where you can get it, and will put you in touch with the appropriate organisation.

Enabling colleagues to practise inclusion

Practising inclusion doesn't mean you have to get 'Mickey the Brickie' in tomorrow to widen your doors and fit a lift. Fine if that's appropriate for your building, but the reality of inclusion is more complex and more subtle, and probably also much easier than turning your working areas into a building site.

As a staff, review your setting together.

- Reassess your furniture to see whether it's suitable for children with, for example, physical problems or sensory difficulties. If you don't have a child at the moment with such difficulties, this can be left until an appropriate time. This doesn't mean, however, waiting until the day before such a child is due to be admitted. The Disability Discrimination Act stipulates a setting's 'anticipatory duty' and so you need to be prepared. As soon as your planning and budget will allow, you should make appropriate adjustments to your building.

- Get some adjustable tables, or a selection of different height surfaces.

- Place tables near natural light, or good quality artificial light. Remember, also, to fit suitable window dressings (curtains, blinds or drapes) that will prevent glare and excessive sunlight coming through, as a child with visual difficulties may be uncomfortable in this situation.

- Make sure that chairs are the right height for a correct posture.

- Have some chairs with arms to support the child in a secure sitting position. This is especially important for the child whose muscle tone is weak – you don't want them toppling off their chair.

- Make spaces between tables and other pieces of furniture to avoid collisions when the children are moving around the room.

- Keep furniture and designated areas in the same place.

- Keep the layout of apparatus the same.

- Don't have polished floors, thus giving a more secure foothold and preventing light reflection. When replacing floor coverings, choose a matt finish for this reason. Also, try to resist the temptation to fit coverings such as laminates, as these can create echoes and excessive noise, thereby causing more difficulties for the child with a hearing problem.

- Keep the floor clear of small items such as pencils, building blocks and so on.

- Have doors that open and close easily, but don't swing back to nip fingers.

- Make sure everybody keeps cupboard doors and drawers closed when not in use.

- If you have steps, fit handrails and/or ramps if necessary. (You can include this in your medium-term planning for redecoration and refurbishment of the setting if there currently aren't any children in the setting who require handrails or ramps. As mentioned above, however, you must show due regard to the 'anticipatory duty' of the Disability Discrimination Act – as soon as practicable you should make appropriate adjustments to your working areas.)

- Make sure the toilets and hand basins are accessible.

- Have a quiet area available at all times. This must be regarded as a pleasant place where the child can go to 'wind down' – it must **never** be used as a 'sin bin' or punishment (in fact, as a staff, re-examine your 'time out' practices and discuss honestly for whose convenience they are in place).

- Display pictures, labels and captions, etc., at the lowest child's height.

- Make sure the day's activities/timetable are displayed in an easy-to-follow time-line displayed at a child's eye level. Make sure it has both pictures and text to enable children of all ability levels to follow the day's proceedings.

- Cover sharp and/or extruding corners with foam.

- Look at your resources, books and equipment.

- Ensure the child who works at floor level has access to the sand and water play by putting the trays on the floor. It's also a fun experience for the able-bodied children, and by all playing together, the children are fully included.

- Use big cushions or beanbags to support the child who works and/or plays at floor level.

- Keep easels and stands in good repair and check they're steady and secure.

- Use jumbo-sized paintbrushes and crayons, etc., or wrap standard-sized handles in foam rubber for the child who has difficulty in holding them.

- Exploit all the child's senses in sand or water play by putting colours and/or scents into sand or water (check with the child's parents/carers first, regarding any allergies, etc.).

- Have some musical instruments that vibrate and others that don't need vision to play. If you have a wooden floor, make it vibrate by stamping or thumping on it. Let the children feel the vibrations with their bare feet or their cheeks.

- Have easy-to-find-and-use door and drawer handles – if you can, have knobs.

- Use Dycem® mats (or similar) to secure small equipment on surfaces.

- Have some persona dolls and books to explore the concept of disability and to develop a positive image of people who have additional needs.

- During story time, circle time or group discussions, use dolls with aids such as spectacles, callipers or a hearing aid, as part of the session.

- Have books with clear, bold images and pictures.

- Read books and stories that feature characters with a disability, but not necessarily as the main character.

- Store books and equipment on shelves that are at a child-friendly height.

- Use tactile materials such as sandpaper, velvet, polystyrene or bubble wrap to make labels, cards, etc.

- Use a variety of balls for catching and throwing games, e.g. with a bell inside, with different surfaces (such as smooth rubber or tennis balls), of different weights, that move erratically, with different smells made by soaking tennis balls in different scents.

- Make sure both the small-play equipment and the outdoor equipment are accessible.

Encourage your colleagues to:

- allocate a key worker to the child; this is enshrined in all the Early Years curricula and is non-negotiable – the child (and their parents/carers) must know who they can approach first with anything, whether it's a quick cuddle at snack time, or a serious talk about a problem within the setting

- speak positively to the child – e.g. 'Come and sit with me, Jaspal, and we'll share this book' will be more effective than 'Sit down and stop doing that, Jaspal'

- speak while facing the child so that they get the whole message without losing either its beginning or its end

- always have a relaxed and warm facial expression

- attract the child's attention by gently touching their shoulder and saying their name before speaking (but remember, you need to be aware of whether the child will tolerate this, and/or, where appropriate, bear the safety and legal issues/implications in mind)

- give instructions in small, easy-to-digest 'bite-size' amounts, if necessary one step at a time

- keep to the daily routine as much as possible

- help the child to achieve their targets using games and other play-based activities

- watch for any personality clashes (whether child–practitioner or child–child) and if necessary change the routine to avoid difficult situations

- maintain a positive and mutually-supportive relationship with the child's parents/carers

- learn to use equipment, communication systems or any other special facilities that the child may have.

You can find a useful framework for developing inclusive practices in *Index for Inclusion: Developing play, learning and participation in early years and childcare*,[1] a publication of the Centre for Studies on Inclusive Education. The *Index* has been circulated to all LAs, primary, secondary and special schools, and should be available from your LA.

In-service training

As SENCO, one of your main roles is to ensure that both you and your colleagues can access appropriate and effective in-service training (INSET) in the field of additional needs. How you achieve this obviously depends on your situation and circumstances. SENCOs from childminding networks, pre-schools or out-of-school clubs, for example, are more likely to receive training in cluster groups, provided by the LA, *SureStart* team or other authority, mainly because this is the most effective way to organise it – a pre-school based in a village hall, meeting twice a week, isn't likely to be in a position to deliver in-house INSET. On the other hand, a SENCO with a specialist qualification in a large primary school could deliver INSET within their school, inviting colleagues from link establishments to join in.

Whatever your situation, it's crucial that the training you obtain for your colleagues and/or yourself is of the highest quality, and is also effective in terms of enabling effective SEN support. Most LAs will offer free training, and you should really take advantage of this. Finance will of course be a factor you have to take into account, but as with all things, training on the cheap may cost you dear in the end. Commission the best you can afford, ensuring it's delivered by a professional with both qualifications and expertise in the field, but also (crucially, I would argue) one who can deliver the training in an interesting, practical and vibrant way. You want to come back from training inspired and enthused, as well as knowledgeable – a day with a provider who bores you out of your box won't ensure that!

You may also find it useful to think about your setting from the inside out – whether you can access in-house training, what type of training is needed, how much, for how long and by whom. Ask yourself the following:

- whether there's somebody on the staff with a specialist qualification who can deliver some training

- what the training needs of your colleagues are

- what's the most urgent type of SEN training required by the majority of the staff, e.g. challenging behaviour, learning difficulties, language and communication difficulties, practising inclusion, etc., and then prioritise these and organise the training as and when you can afford it

- what the requirements of the children with additional needs are in terms of the expertise of the staff supporting them

- how training places can be allocated on a 'needs first' basis

- where you can get funding for the training

- whether there are any outside sources of extra funding for training (ask your Area SENCO/Inclusion Consultant) – remember, your LA will probably offer free good quality training so just ask.

Once you've spent precious finances on training, it's vital you evaluate what happened and whether you had value for money. Most authorities, establishments and training providers will issue evaluation sheets to training participants, so ask for copies of these to help with your evaluation. This feedback will enable you to make an informed decision about future training plans. Figure 3.1 shows a typical Evaluation Form.

From the overall opinion of the participants, you'll be able to judge whether your money was well spent, whether you'd commission the same provider/trainer again, whether the training can be put into practice effectively in your setting, whether you can share and/or cascade the training for wider benefit, and so on.

Depending on the size of your setting, you might also choose to keep a record of who's received what training, when, etc. Figure 3.2 illustrates the type of Summary Form you could use for this.

COURSE EVALUATION

Course title:_____

To what extent did the course meet its objectives?

Please comment on the process of the course: e.g. the presentation, the activities, the balance of activities.

If you were running the course, is there anything you might add or omit?

REFLECTION AND ACTION PLANNING

In what ways do you think the children could benefit from your attendance at this course?

What could you/the setting do to ensure they get the benefits?

What could be the steps to achieving that?

 Figure 3.1   Course Evaluation Form

A Summary Form like the one in Figure 3.2 can prove very useful in identifying whether there's a fair distribution of training opportunities across the staff, a balanced choice of training courses so that all areas requiring development are addressed, and if value for money has been achieved. You can also judge whether a picture is building up of any single provider receiving consistently poor or consistently positive evaluations, thus helping you to make informed choices in your future planning. Your setting may already incorporate this information into the individual practitioner files, which are available for parents/carers, Ofsted inspectors and visitors to look at. There's a blank version of the form on the CD-ROM.

DELIVERING IN-SERVICE SEN/INCLUSION TRAINING

If you find that you're 'It' in your setting (i.e. the designated trainer) rather than buying-in the training, you may find the materials on the CD-ROM with this book to be of use. They offer the basis of three mini-courses that you can adapt to suit yourself or use as they stand. They are available in both a downloadable format and as PowerPoint presentations from which you can print the slides for handouts.

Name	Date of training	Course attended	Purpose of course	Provider	Value (scale 1–10)
Ann Scott	12.11.09	SEN Code of Practice in Practice	Principles of using CoP	Adam Smith Training Associates	10 – excellent day
May Howard	12/19/26 Jan. 10 & 2 Feb. 10	Encouraging Positive Behaviour in the Early Years	Strategies to work with children with behavioural difficulties	Riddesdale LA EBD Support Service	5 – average content; poor delivery
Don Smith	15.01.10	Role of the SENCO	SENCO training	Riddesdale LA SEN Support Service	9 – good delivery; good content
Ann Scott	13/20/27 Feb. 10	Lang. Lit. & Comm. for EY Children with additional needs	Strategies for teaching language & literacy skills	Riddesdale LA Literacy Advisers & University of Riddesdale	8 – very useful; good content; delivery so-so

Figure 3.2   Record of staff SEN training

CD-ROM Resources for this chapter

Figure 3.1   Course Evaluation Form

Figure 3.2   Record of Staff SEN training

Special Educational Needs Code of Practice 1–5

Who's Who and What's What of SEN 1–5

Helping to Identify Children with Additional Needs 1–15

Planning Effective Interventions 1–5

Useful websites

The Training and Development Agency for Schools:
http://www.tda.gov.uk/

Department for Children, Schools and Families
http://www.dcsf.gov.uk/

Both of these websites are worth looking at in depth as they have loads of links and downloads that are very useful.

Centre for Studies on Inclusive Education (for the Index for Inclusion and other related matters):
http://www.csie.org.uk/publications/inclusion–index-explained.shtml

Note

1 *Index for Inclusion: Developing play, learning and participation in early years and childcare,* T. Booth, M. Ainscow, and D. Kingston (Centre for Studies on Inclusive Education, 2006). See also *Further Reading* for details of how to obtain a copy.

4

Supporting the children – making sure their entitlements are met

The **key points** covered in this chapter are:

- Identifying a difficulty and expressing concern.
- The three phases of the *Special Educational Needs (SEN) Code of Practice* (Early Years Action, Early Years Action Plus, Statutory Assessment) and the SENCO's role in each phase.
- The practicalities of planning, writing and using Individual Education Plans (IEPs).
- Organising and holding reviews – some suggestions and ideas.

INTRODUCTION

Here we'll be exploring the issues surrounding the core of this book: the child. 'Catching' em young' and supporting them fully are their entitlements. As practitioners responsible for helping the little ones in our care to achieve their potential, we must strive to become experts and use that expertise professionally.

As professionals, we are here for the child – the child is not here for us.

Throughout this chapter, I will refer to sample *pro formae* to use at the various stages of supporting the child with additional needs. Do check first whether your LA has its own set of these and whether they should be used in preference to any 'home grown' versions. As with all suggested paperwork in this book, the forms on offer can be tweaked to suit your situation, so in the unlikely event of your LA not have locally-standardised *pro formae*, you can use my suggestions as a basis to design your own.

HELPING TO IDENTIFY A DIFFICULTY

If the child's key worker has a concern about a child, they should do the following:

- ask the child's parents/carers for permission to speak to you as SENCO

- observe and assess the child, recording the results objectively (you should be familiar with the sections on observations in the EYFS or your local equivalent documents)

- complete a form expressing their concerns, involving the parents/carers in this

- differentiate the child's curriculum or learning programme

- monitor and record the child's progress closely, informing both the parents/carers and you of any outcomes

- review, together with the parents/carers and you, whether and when the child needs to move to Early Years Action.

Observations will highlight what the child can do, and should be done in a variety of situations – for example, self-chosen activities, structured activities, adult-led activities and play activities – thereby building up a picture of the child's achievements and abilities. Use the information to assess the child's general achievement level, and to plan their next targets. Share the information with everyone involved, helping them gain a fuller insight into the child's abilities. You'll find a more detailed discussion of observations in Chapter 5

EXPRESSING CONCERN

Make sure the child's parents/carers are happy with what you've written on the Expression of Concern Form. Some parents/carers may feel anxious or threatened so try not to make it stressful for them. Avoid words like 'register' or 'official', which may have negative associations. This might be the beginning of a long-term partnership between you and the parents/carers, and it's important from the outset that they trust you and have confidence in you.

Figure 4.1 shows an example of a completed Expression of Concern Form.

 There's a blank version of the form on the CD-ROM that accompanies this book.

Differentiated learning plans

The child's curriculum should be differentiated to support their learning. Adapt the activities, presentation, teaching styles, timing and so on, enabling the child to achieve the target skill or concept. Break down the final target into small steps, done one at a time and thoroughly consolidated, before moving on to the next one. Thus the child learns via a graduated approach, allowing for their personal learning style and level. Record the plan on a form such as the example of a completed Differentiated Learning Plan Form shown in Figure 4.2.

 There's a blank copiable version of the form on the CD-ROM.

EARLY YEARS ACTION

If you're still worried about the child, despite their differentiated curriculum, then move to Early Years Action, by planning, writing and implementing an IEP for the child, practitioner and parents/carers to work from. (You can also involve the parents/carers by designing a Play Plan together. This is a framework for the parents/carers to follow up at home the work you're doing in the setting. Its

Expression of Concern Form	
Name of setting: Dales View Nursery	**Child's name**: Kieran Smith
Date of Birth: 18.04.05	**Date of admission:** 13.03.09
Area(s) of concern: Lack of social interaction with adults & children	
Area(s) of learning affected [tick boxes as appropriate]:	
Personal, social and emotional development ☑	Physical development ☐
Communication, language and literacy ☑	Creative development ☐
Mathematical development ☐	Knowledge and understanding of the world ☐
Date(s) of observation(s): 14/16/19 Apr. 09 **Type of observation:** Focused (15 mins)	
Findings of observation(s): Kieran's lack of interaction occurred mainly in the work areas (especially when he was in smaller groups) and the playground. He usually refused to join in singing or action rhymes, or to answer other children's questions/invitations to play. He seemed to be reluctant to use the toys or books except when he was alone. His play was usually solitary.	
Date(s) of assessment(s): None yet done	**Assessment(s) used:**
Findings of assessment(s):	
Action taken: Key worker allocated to Kieran to support him during group sessions and help him to achieve specific objectives from the Early Years Foundation Stage (see Kieran's Small steps planning form).	
Have the parents/carers been consulted? Yes/~~No~~	**Parent's/Carer's signature:** Annie Smith
Has the SENCO been consulted? Yes/~~No~~ (told but not yet involved)	
Signed: Clare Hampton	**Position:** Early years practitioner
Date: 20.04.09	**Date review due:** 20.07.09

Figure 4.1   An example of a completed Expression of Concern Form

targets are linked with those of the IEP, and the supporting activities are always play-oriented, with lots of games and fun things to do. There's a fuller discussion of Play Plans in Chapter 6.)

Remember – *it is not your role to implement every child's IEP*, unless you're the child's key worker. There's a common misperception that it's the SENCO's job to teach the child or work with them on the IEP, regardless of who the child's primary practitioner is. Try to resist any pressure on you to take this on – you have enough to do in implementing the IEPs of 'your' children, as well as fulfilling your other roles as SENCO.

If you *are* experiencing this type of difficulty, ask your manager or head to support you by explaining your role and position to the other practitioners in the setting. Show them the relevant parts of the *SEN Code of Practice* to highlight your point – see Section 4:16. (Make sure, however, that your colleagues are receiving the support and help *they* need. It's possible they're pressuring you to 'do' the IEPs because they're feeling insecure, threatened or de-skilled, and would appreciate some help themselves.)

Differentiated Learning Plan		
Child's name: Mary Ann Jones	**Area of concern:** Self-help skills	
Area of Learning: Personal, social and emotional development		
Learning Objective/EYFS Scale target:		
Dress and undress independently and manage their own personal hygiene		
Small steps to objective:	**Date achieved**	**Date checked**
1. Mary Ann will put on her coat with help from a supporter before each playtime. She will fasten the final button after the supporter has put her arms into the sleeves & shown her how to fasten the other buttons.	13.02.09	17.02.09
2. Mary Ann will fasten the last button when dressing up in the Home Comer, after the helper has put her arms into the sleeves & done the other buttons.	17.02.09	20.02.09
3. Mary Ann will fasten the last two buttons of her coat each time she puts it on, after a helper has put her arms into the sleeves & done the other buttons.	20.02.09	24.02.09
4. Mary Ann will fasten half of her coat buttons after the helper has put her arms into the sleeves & done the other buttons.	27.02.09	
5. Mary Ann will fasten all her buttons independently when dressing.		
6. Mary Ann will put her arms into her coat before going out.		
Equipment and materials: Button-matching game; Mary Ann's clothes; button-fastening game; dressing up clothes		
Staff involved: Clare Hampton and Maria Davies (daily sessions)		
Home support/follow-up: We have asked Mary Ann's Mum to put Mary Ann's buttoned coat on rather than her zipped one. We'll also practise with the buttons in her other garments (cardigans, blouses, etc.). Mary Ann takes home the button-matching game to play with over the weekends.		

Figure 4.2   An example of a completed Differentiated Learning Form

IEPs are decided by the practitioner, the child's parents/carers, you as SENCO (although if you're not the key worker, your input will be limited) and, if possible, the child, at a level that's appropriate for them. Their age isn't important since even very young children can be involved. For example, they could choose from selected equipment or decide from several options of activity. There isn't a shortcut to planning IEPs, which are unique and specific to each child – there's a good reason why they're called *Individual* Education Plans!

The IEP should target the child's difficulties from the point of view of their strengths. Don't overload the child when you choose their targets – the *SEN Code* says a *maximum* of three or four targets, so you can choose only as many as the child can manage. If this means only one or two, then that's fine – just note this down on the IEP. Choose the targets according to the child's needs and achievement level and, where possible, link them with the relevant curriculum goals or targets.

Always select the targets from the point that the child has already reached and has experienced success with.

Here are a few handy hints for planning IEPs:

- write down the targets concisely, avoiding jargon

- specify how you'll know when the child has achieved the target and make the criteria achievable to avoid failure – you can always make the criteria tougher if the child achieves them too easily

- decide the 'rewards' to acknowledge and celebrate success and let the child choose – rewards must be meaningful for them – and to avoid creating a distinction between 'work' and 'play', never use a 'play' session as a reward

- record when the child's performance was checked, by whom and with what result – these details are very important and may be crucial at a later stage

- celebrate the child's strengths as this is vital to avoid getting bogged down in what they can't do – there'll be lots of things that they *can* do, and do well, so try to acknowledge these

- check the targets already achieved – they may need to be taught again or revised – and never move the child on until they've consolidated their earlier skills

- if an IEP is failing the child, try again with new ideas – this is part of professionalism, to have the integrity to acknowledge that a plan isn't working and then change it.

Figure 4.3. shows an example of a completed IEP Form.

There's a blank copiable version of the form on the accompanying CD-ROM.

In the meantime, you as SENCO will have other responsibilities:

- Tell the child's parents/carers about the Local Authority (LA)'s Parent Partnership Service (PPS) and give them all the LA's available information. For non-English speakers, contact the translation services offered by the LA's PPS.

- Collect all the setting's information about the child. Don't involve volunteers who come into the setting, particularly if they're non-professionals. Their input can only be anecdotal and won't have any legal standing. Above all, the child's right to confidentiality must be respected and protected, and volunteers must not have access to private information regarding the child's difficulties.

- Collect any relevant information from outside agents who may be involved, such as a social worker or the health visitor.

- If appropriate, liaise with the educational psychologist (EP). This may only be on a 'need to know' basis and must be done *with the parent's/carer's*

Individual Education Plan	
Child's name: Harry Jones	**DOB:** 29.03.04
Date IEP implemented: 13.01.09	**Code of Practice level:** E Y Action
Areas of strength: Harry enjoys books; he paints excellent pictures.	
Areas of difficulty: Harry has difficulty with early number work. He has hearing problems – he's got grommets; he regularly attends the ear, nose & throat department at the hospital.	
Targets to be reached by: 8.04.09	
1) Harry will be able to count from 1 to 4 using apparatus.	
2) Harry will be able to recognise and name 1 to 4 when shown in written form.	
3) Harry will be able to write any numeral from 1 to 4 on request.	
Criteria for success:	
1) Harry will count from 1 to 4 using four different types of apparatus, 4 times out of 5.	
2) Harry will recognise and name 1, 2, 3 or 4 in written form in a variety of places 4 times out of 5.	
3) Harry will correctly write a requested numeral from 1 to 4, 4 times out of 5.	
Teaching methods: initially in a one-to-one situation in the quiet area; then in the main nursery areas to use counting displays, posters, name tags, etc.	
Staff involved: Mrs Smith, early years teacher; Mrs Scott, nursery nurse; Mrs Jones, mother, to work at home.	
Frequency of programme: twice daily (morning and afternoon) for a maximum of ten minutes, five days per week; once per evening at home when possible.	
Equipment/Apparatus: cubes, counters, plastic sorting shapes, any appropriate counting apparatus of Harry's choice, paper, pencils and felt-tip pens.	
Date of next review: 9.04.09	
To be attended by Mrs Smith, Mrs Scott & Mrs Jones.	

Figure 4.3   An example of a completed IEP form

permission. If they're anxious about it, be sure to handle the situation with great sensitivity.

- Arrange a review meeting at least once every three months. You may need to do this more often, say every six weeks or so, depending on the situation and the child's age.

IEP reviews

Forward planning, organisation and a shared but confidential calendar or diary in the setting can result in successful reviews. As SENCO, you're responsible for organising the reviews that are held at the earlier levels of SEN provision. (The LA usually coordinates the Annual Review of Statements.) Here are some practical suggestions for planning a review.

- Put trigger-reminders in the diary, working backwards from the review date. Plan about four weeks before the review date and jot down a note on each appropriate date, for the things you need to do. For example:

12.03.09   (i.e. four weeks ahead) Walter Smith's review due on 8.04.09. Request information and advice from:
Walter's parents and Walter
Mrs Dodd (early years teacher)
Mrs Jones (nursery nurse)
Mr Muir (educational psychologist)
Advice to be received by 26.03.09.
22.03.09   (i.e. two and a half weeks ahead) Advice received so far from Mrs Dodd, Mrs James.
Remind Mr & Mrs Smith and Mr Muir that advice is due by 26.03.09.
26.03.09 |(i.e. two weeks ahead) Send out invitations & advice documents for Walter Smith's review.
7.04.09   (i.e. the day before) Get coffee, biscuits and flowers for Walter Smith's review.
8.04.09   Walter Smith's review: 10.00 a.m.

- If English isn't the parents'/carers' first language, arrange for an interpreter. Make sure they have been CRB checked and offer an excellent level of translation, to ensure accuracy of information. Your LA should have its own bank of approved translators, so check with them first.

- If the parents/carers use an alternative system of communication ask them whether they'd like support in any way. Your LA may have a bank of signers or alternative communication system users who can help. If you're unsure, check with your Area SENCO.

- On the review day, make the room cheerful and welcoming, with coffee and biscuits and some flowers. Help the parents/carers to relax by inviting them in a few minutes earlier.

- Arrange the chairs in a circle, with a low table in the middle. Some parents/carers will feel threatened or intimidated by the review, so don't organise the room as if for a formal interview.

- Work your way through the Review Form systematically, helping to keep everybody focused on each point as it comes up for discussion.

- Ask for the key worker's contribution, which is crucial, as they will know the child most intimately within the setting.

- Invite the other agents' contributions, if relevant.

- Ensure that the parents/carers and the child, if appropriate, can offer their input. You could design a Parent's Review Form to give to the parents/carers some time before the review and which will help them focus on what they want to say in the meeting.

Figure 4.4 on page 44 shows an example of a completed Parent's Review Form, and you'll find a blank version of the form on the CD-ROM.

If the child isn't there but is able to make a contribution to the discussion, they can do this through the parents/carers on a Child's Review Form. Encourage the child to record on it what they think about the IEP, their progress and so on. Talk through the form with the parents/carers and make sure they are happy about completing it. Figure 4.5 on page 45 shows an example of a completed Child's Review Form.

There's a blank copiable Child's Review Form on the CD-ROM.

During the review:

- Make sure that everybody has time to speak but don't let people hog the lime-light. As Chair, you can bring the focus back to the discussion and give the other people present a chance to have their say.

- Include a plan of further action. On the Review Form, you can record this as a simple *Yes/No* deletion.

- Conclude by briefly summarising what was said, asking whether everybody agrees. Clear up any misunderstandings immediately and ask everybody to initial your notes before they leave.

- Book the date of the next review immediately.

- Sign and date the Review Form. If possible, give the parents/carers a copy immediately.

- Have a quiet word with the parents/carers to make sure they're happy with the review's outcome. This is especially important for parents/carers who are shy, or who feel upset or threatened by the process. They may need to have some of the paperwork explained to them, especially if they have language and/or literacy difficulties themselves. Make sure you do this sensitively and in a supportive way.

- Circulate copies of the Review Form to everybody who has attended the meet-ing as soon as possible so that any queries can be clarified more or less straight away. Also send a copy to the relevant people who didn't attend.

Figure 4.6 on page 46 provides an example of a completed Review Form.

You will find a blank version of the form on the CD-ROM.

You must monitor the child between reviews in case the IEP isn't working. If you think you've done some poor or unhelpful planning, it's crucial that you act imme-diately. Call an interim review to discuss your concerns with the parents/carers and any other staff involved, and then change the IEP.

EARLY YEARS ACTION PLUS

This is the stage when you ask for the advice of an outside specialist. You will usually refer to outside agents when your setting isn't able to offer the expertise needed to

Parent's Review Form
Name of child: Sadie Hampton   **Date of child's birth:** 9.01.03
Your child's health: **Is your child usually healthy?** Yes apart from her asthma
Do they take any medicines? If so, what are they? Inhaler mostly in winter
Have these changed within the last two months? No
Your child at home: **Does your child have any hobbies?** She goes to Brownies
What does your child enjoy doing at home? Playing with her dolls & helping me bake
What does your child need help with at home? Her reading and numbers
Your child in <u>Catton Lea Nursery School</u> **Is your child happy to come to our setting?** Usually
Are you happy about the way we support your child in the setting? Yes
Are you pleased with your child's progress? Yes
Do you have any worries about your child's Individual Education Plan (IEP)? If so, what? I think she needs to do more work on her reading
Is there anything you think we need to change? If so, what? I think her targets should be easier because she still isn't reading
What's next for your child?
Are you happy with the targets on your child's IEP? Yes – I think it's important to concentrate on her reading and maths work
What do you think your child should learn next? More concentration – I think she needs to learn to keep her head down
Do you have any questions to ask at the review? Who are you going to contact about Sadie? Will we be able to come to the meetings? Will she have to leave Catton Lea? I don't want her going to a special school

Figure 4.4   An example of a completed Parent's Review Form

manage the child's difficulties. The multi-agency approach widens here, with everybody benefiting from a broader spectrum of information. Everyone should cooperate closely, with regular liaison, to ensure seamless and better quality provision. The *SEN Code of Practice* gives useful general guidelines about why and when you should refer a child to an outside agent (Section 4:31).

Child's Review Form

My name is Marco Camilleri

I was born on 12 September 2003

I like playing football. I like making models and dressing up in the home corner.

I worry about reading and the computer. Sometimes Mrs Scott shouts at me.

For my next IEP, I want to do more games like I play with Mrs Scott to help me with my letter matching. I like the bingo on the computer.

Parent's signature Antonio Camilleri

Date 19 May 2009

Figure 4.5   An example of a completed Child's Review Form

Outside agents

External professionals include the following:

- *The LA's support services for learning difficulties, speech and language difficulties, visual and hearing impairment and physical disabilities.* These can provide advice on teaching techniques and strategies, setting management, curriculum materials, curriculum development, direct teaching or practical support for practitioners, part-time specialist help, or access to learning support assistance. You should have contact details for these services. If not, the SEN section of your LA will be able to supply them, or your inclusion consultant will be able to advise you. If your setting is private or non-maintained, link up with your local state-maintained early years providers to share information, facilities, services and best practice.

- *The child or educational psychology services,* which can carry out more specialised assessments, suggest problem-solving strategies (including techniques in managing behaviour) and evaluate individual children's progress. They can also offer information and advice about the development of your SEN policy and assist with professional development in the area of SEN, as well as helping to promote inclusion.

IEP Review Form	
Child's name: John Davies	**DOB:** 31.01.04
Level: Early Years Action/~~Early Years Action Plus~~ [delete as appropriate]	
Date of review: 9.04.09	~~1st~~/2nd/3rd review [delete as appropriate]
Present at review: Mr & Mrs Davies (parents/carers) Mrs Simpson (teacher) Mrs Frampton (SENCO)	
Report of child's progress/IEP: 1) John can count three items of a variety of apparatus correctly; he still needs to count from 1. 2) John can recognise and name 1 & 2 when shown in written form in a variety of places. 3) John can write 1 & 2 when asked. The targets have still to be achieved and the criteria need to be reduced. John continues to have difficulties both at home and in the setting.	
Additional comments/reports from people not present: a) Mrs Davies read out John's opinion (see attached Child's Review Form). John has been happier since the IEP was put in place and he enjoys doing his activities. He says it is hard though and he thinks that his targets are too difficult because he can't remember his work from the day before. b) Mrs O'Halloran (nursery nurse) reports that John concentrates well but has difficulty in retaining the concept for longer than a few minutes (see attached detailed report). c)	
Further action: Adjust targets to learn numbers 1–3. SENCO to request input from Early Years Learning Support Service.	
Continue with IEP?	Yes/~~No~~
Modify IEP?	Yes/~~No~~
Remain at present stage?	~~Yes~~/No
Move to next stage?	Yes/~~No~~
Discontinue SEN procedure?	~~Yes~~/No
Other action?	Yes/~~No~~ (See 'Further action' above)
Next review due: 21.05.09 (6 weeks)	
Name: A. FRAMPTON (SENCO)	**Signed:** A. Frampton
Date: 9.04.09	

Figure 4.6   An example of a completed IEP Review Form

- *The behaviour support service.*

- *Advisers or teachers of information and communication technology (ICT) for children with additional needs.*

- *Social services.*

- *Child protection services.*

- *Medical services,* including health visitors (HVs), paediatric nurses and/or paediatricians, nurses, community or hospital-based paediatricians, child psychiatrists, general practitioners (GPs), physiotherapists, speech and language therapists, occupational therapists and hospital-based counsellors. If a child arrives with an identified problem, any combination of these professionals is likely to be already involved. If you identify a difficulty, after consulting with the child's parents/carers, you'll probably have to liaise initially with the local HV or the child's GP.

- *Private and voluntary organisations*, which are a valuable source of help and information.

You must establish positive and cooperative relations with these agencies. They're very important for the early identification of difficulties and for advising you on effective strategies aimed at preventing further problems developing. As well as these mutual benefits of shared expertise, the liaison and cooperative approach will become a normal part of your policy on special educational needs long before you need to call agents in. The multi-agency approach should be child-centred and flexible, making sure that support for the child continues to be appropriate, even when their needs change.

BUYER BEWARE!

- If you decide to commission freelance or private specialists or organisations, there are several serious considerations to keep in mind. You (or your setting's manager or head) must check the qualifications and experience of the agents you buy in. You must also make sure that all police checks and clearances have been done, and be aware that your setting, rather than the LA, will usually have to pay for these outside agents or services.

- If parents/carers share with you reports, assessments or other information about the child that they themselves have commissioned from private providers, make sure you check the credentials of that provider before you rely on their documentation.

Making a referral

As SENCO, it's more than likely you'll have to make the referral. However, you, the key practitioner, the child's parents/carers and, where possible, the child will have already decided that this is the plan of action. After you've asked for outside help, you'll be responsible for *coordinating* the SEN provision made for the child and for any decisions made about this. (NB: *coordinating* the provision – not necessarily *providing* or implementing it, unless you're the key worker or named practitioner.)

Your LA should have a set procedure for maintained settings to make referrals to outside agents. Private and voluntary settings should link up with their local early years establishments to find out about the procedure and to take advantage of the advice and support on offer. There are several things you should do before actually sending a referral to an outside specialist.

- Hold a review with the child's parents/carers and, if possible, the child. Discuss the IEPs and the child's progress (or lack of it), ask for the parents'/carers' and the child's views and decide if you need more information for the referral. Record on the Review Form that you're going to make a referral and to whom.

- Everybody should agree what's to be included on the Referral Form. Use blank copies of the form at the review meeting to draft the main points of the referral. As SENCO, you'll be completing the form, so it's important that you have all the necessary information and everyone's agreement before the meeting finishes.

- Collect all the relevant information that the outside agent will need (e.g. the IEPs, the review forms, records of observations, assessments or profiles, samples of the child's work that can illustrate their difficulties) to give an overview of the child and their problems. Don't involve volunteers or helpers in this information-gathering process.

- Complete the Referral Form and, together with all the appropriate records and information, send it to the outside agent involved.

Figure 4.7 shows an example of a completed Referral Form.

 You'll find a blank version of the form on the CD-ROM.

The outside agent will meet with the key practitioner, yourself, the parents/carers and the child if possible. They may also want to make a preliminary assessment of the child. This will be more specialised than any you will have done, and will focus more specifically on the child's difficulties.

At the initial meeting you'll have a chance to draw on the advice and suggestions made by the specialist and to plan a new IEP together with them. This should incorporate some of the strategies and suggestions made by the specialist. It's crucial that the parents/carers and the child get the chance to contribute to the planning of the IEP. They won't have the agent's specialised knowledge, but they will have their own expertise to offer. For example, they'll be able to say whether a proposed method of incentive-and-reward will work, whether a target is attractive and whether the activities are exciting – all important considerations if the new IEP is to work.

The implementation of the new IEP is done by the child, the parents/carers and the key practitioner, with you overseeing its implementation. Usually the outside specialist will monitor the programme and offer ongoing advice. How often they visit will depend on such things as their workload, the seriousness of the child's difficulties, and the amount of support you will need.

Your other responsibilities as SENCO will continue in the meantime.

- Make sure the child's parents/carers are still completely involved and informed about their child's progress (you must tell them of any unscheduled visits made by the outside specialist and what was discussed).

- Relay any advice and support from the external agent to both the child's key worker and their parents/carers.

Child's name: Sarah James	DOB: 18.04.02
Date of referral: 14.08.09	Name of setting: Catton Lea Nursery
Name of main practitioner: Polly Carlton	
Name of SENCO: Maria Dwyer	
Area(s) of concern [tick boxes as appropriate]:	
Personal, social and emotional development ☑	Physical development ☐
Communication, language and literacy ☐	Creative development ☐
Mathematical development ☐	Knowledge and understanding of the world ☐
Have IEPs been put in place? Yes/~~No~~	Are copies of IEPs enclosed? Yes/~~No~~

If not, please state reason
If other records/documents are enclosed, please state what: Examples of Sarah's paintings; Foundation Stage profile
Has the SENCO been involved? Yes/~~No~~
Have the parents/carers/carers been involved? ~~Yes~~/No
If not, please state reason: Sarah's parents/carers did not want *to* be involved with doing the IEPs at home.
Has the child been involved? Yes/~~No.~~
If not, please state reason:
Reason(s) for referral (this should be signed by each practitioner who makes a contribution): Sarah's concentration span is no more than one or two minutes – she finds difficulty in staying on task with any single activity for longer than 35 seconds. Her maximum time is when she is doing a jigsaw. Her play is usually solitary and she finds it difficult to be in group situations without becoming aggressive towards one of the other children. IEPs targeting these difficulties haven't helped Sarah develop positive behaviour and we need more specialised advice and support. We are concerned that her paintings and drawings are almost always about crying children.
Polly Carlton (Nursery Nurse)
Signature of referring practitioner: Marie Dwyer Position: SENCO
Signature of parent/carer: Ann James

Figure 4.7   An example of a completed Referral Form

- Liaise with the specialist agent(s), the child's key worker and their parents/carers to monitor the new IEP, the targets, and the teaching strategies – you'll then be able to act swiftly if the IEP is failing to support the child.

- Ensure that the IEP is reviewed at least every three months/once per term, remembering that you can call an interim meeting if there's a serious concern to discuss.

- Ensure the records of the new IEPs are kept up to date and carefully maintained so if the child is eventually referred for a Statutory Assessment, the LA will ask you for evidence of the differentiated work done with the child – the IEPs will form the main body of this strand of the evidence.

STATUTORY ASSESSMENT

Between 1 and 2 per cent of children will continue to cause concern and those involved may decide to refer the child to the LA for a Statutory Assessment. The three main sources of referral are: early years settings, the child's parents/carers, or other agencies.

Early years settings

If your setting is delivering funded education, whether maintained or in receipt of private or government funding (and this includes accredited networks of childminders), you will have a statutory right to refer a child for assessment if the child is three years or older. Otherwise you can ask the parents/carers to request a statutory assessement (see the following section).

Parents/carers

Parents/carers may decide to refer their child for a Statutory Assessment. The LA must then carry out the request:

- unless a Statutory Assessment has already been done on the child in the six months before the referral or

- unless the LA feels the assessment is unnecessary having considered all the evidence supplied in support of the referral.

The LA must inform you if the parents/carers have made a referral and they must decide within six weeks of a referral whether they will carry out the assessment. Where you and the parents/carers have been working together, you've probably agreed to the parental referral. Sometimes, however, the parents/carers may be unhappy about the way the setting has dealt with their child's difficulties and they might then decide to make the referral independently. When this happens, the LA must consider the referral and take appropriate action.

Other agencies

This is usually done by a professional from health or social services, and typically concerns a child under five who has complex or profound difficulties. The

LA will collect evidence in the same way as they do for referrals via education professionals.

How is a referral made?

There's a standard procedure to follow, normally entailing you working with the educational psychologist (EP) who will advise you on completing the forms and gathering the required documentation. The referral itself is usually made on the LA's official form. You must include:

- the parents'/carers' views, as recorded on earlier review forms (they may also like to send an additional statement)

- the child's views from the review records, but also through an involvement of the child in the actual referral process

- copies of all the IEPs

- evidence of the child's progress (e.g. records of achievement, profiles, etc.)

- other relevant records, information or advice on health-related matters from the HV, the child's GP or the speech and language therapist

- the reports by, and evidence of the involvement of, outside agents

- evidence to show to what extent you have actually followed the advice of the outside agents.

Statutory Assessment procedure

Next, you must send the whole package to the LA, which must decide within six weeks whether to go ahead with a Statutory Assessment of the child. The LA is obliged to write to the parents/carers outlining the procedures involved in deciding on an assessment, informing them of their rights, advising them about the PPS, and asking whether they would like the LA to consult any other professionals if an assessment goes ahead.

Within this six-week period, the child's parents/carers will have 29 days to inform the LA whether or not they agree with the referral going ahead. If they do agree, they don't have to wait for the 29 days to expire but can tell the LA at the beginning so they can start the process immediately.

Sometimes the LA will turn down a request for a Statutory Assessment and if so, they must write to the child's parents/carers and you, giving the reasons as to why this has happened. The parents/carers will have the right to appeal to an SEN tribunal if they disagree with the LA's decision.

Once the LA has decided to make a Statutory Assessment they have to follow a strict timetable. There's a useful flow chart of this in the *SEN Code of Practice* on page 120. (Spot the spelling mistake at the point where the LA decides whether to assess the child!) The LA must complete the process within the ten weeks following, because they must then decide whether to start the next stage, which is the issuing of a Statement of Special Educational Needs.

At the start of the assessment process, the LA will contact the child's parents/carers, all the professionals involved with the child, and the EP for their opinions and advice regarding the child's current progress.

You and the key worker will have an overview of the child's achievements in relation to their peer group and the Early Years Foundation Stage or your local equivalent curriculum. You'll know which strategies were successful and which were less effective, how the child performed, what they found difficult and what they achieved. You'll also know what the child's learning styles are, how they react to certain activities or situations in the setting, and how they interact with the other children.

If the child is a baby, you will probably be liaising with the other agencies in the referral. Use the Common Assessment Framework, or your local equivalent, to help you focus on the areas of concern even though you will have to submit the LA's own referral form ultimately.

Completing the educational advice

The LA will send you forms for the educational advice. If you're doing this for the first time, don't worry – you'll have all the information you need in the child's records. To help focus your thoughts, and to bring together some of the information, think about the following questions:

Communication and language skills
Does the child:

- Communicate by speech, gestures, oral sounds or not at all?

- Make eye contact during conversations?

- Speak clearly?

- Always communicate or just sometimes?

- Communicate with adults, or the other children, or both, or neither?

- Understand what is said to them?

- Talk about everything, or just a few topics, or only one?

- Use the kind of language expected from a child of that age?

- Play imaginatively?

- Speak English as their main language? If not, what language is spoken at home?

Social, emotional and personal skills
Does the child:

- Interact well with the other children?

- Have difficulties with relationships with the adults in the setting?

- Share and take turns appropriately?

- Get easily upset over small things?

- Play happily with other children?

- Play happily alone?

- Have a reasonable concentration span?

- Have any ritualistic or obsessive behaviours (e.g. hand flapping, spinning the wheels on toys, doing the same jigsaw time after time)?

- Become distressed at any change in the routine?

- Join in group activities and discussions confidently?

- Have self-help skills (i.e. are they independent at the toilet, at meals or at dressing)?

Physical skills
Does the child:

- Have any physical difficulties?

- Have well-developed gross fine motor skills (i.e. can they run, jump, climb, kick a ball, ride a tricycle, hop, skip, etc.)?

- Have well-developed fine motor skills (i.e. can they manipulate puzzles, do threading or cutting with scissors, use pencils, crayons or paintbrushes, etc.)?

- Have good eyesight?

- Have good hearing?

Learning abilities
Does the child:

- Have difficulties in learning (e.g. with early literacy skills or early mathematical concepts)?

- Need lots of repetition and practice before learning a concept?

- Seem to learn something one day and forget it the next? Does this happen fairly often?

- Predict the next part of a story?

- Try to solve problems?

- Make simple decisions?

- Show curiosity about how things work?

- Have an interest in the world around them?

Medical and health issues
Does the child:

- Have any known medical condition or disability?

- Have any allergies?

- Have any special dietary needs?

- Need to take medication on a regular basis?

- Have any sensory disability (e.g. visual or hearing)?

- Have any physical disability?

- Have prolonged absences for medical reasons?

A Statutory Assessment of a child doesn't always result in the writing of a Statement of Special Educational Needs since the LA may decide not to proceed. If so, they must write to both the child's parents/carers and you, explaining why, within two weeks of the completion of the assessment and the making of the decision. They must also outline what provision they think is appropriate to meet the child's needs. Once again, the parents/carers have the right of appeal to the SEN Tribunal if they disagree with the LA's decision.

However, the LA may decide to write and issue a Statement of Special Educational Needs, a legally-binding document outlining the areas of difficulty being experienced by the child, and the most appropriate provision for meeting their needs. They have to send a draft copy of the Statement to the parents/carers within the same time limit of two weeks, and the final Statement must be written and issued within eight weeks from that point.

In other words, the entire process from initial referral to Statement must not take any longer than 26 weeks.

Once the final Statement has been written, a copy of it must be sent to the child's parents/carers together with details of their right to appeal to the SEN Tribunal, if they disagree with anything in the Statement.

Annual/Biannual review

A Statement of Special Educational Needs is formally reviewed annually, but if the child is under five, it's reviewed every six months. This is to ensure that the recommendations made in the Statement are still applicable and appropriate. The six-monthly (Biannual) Review isn't as formal or full as the main annual review. The *SEN Code of Practice* enables the Statement to be amended if necessary, at the Biannual Review.

Involving the child

Involving the child in their own planning and decision-making helps them to feel confident and happy about the process they've become a part of. Sometimes they'll need help to express their views and opinions, but this doesn't lessen the importance of what they have to say. Thankfully, this is enshrined in the statutory Early Years documents which recognise the paramount right of the child to be heard and listened to when decisions are being made that affect their development and progress. It is crucial that your setting embraces this and ensures the child's views (on all matters) are taken into account, and respected, from the moment they enter the setting to the day they move on.

- Develop an ethos where individual differences are accepted and respected. Have resources and books that reflect a wide range of abilities and regularly share these with all the children.

- Talk to the child about their difficulties and why they're being assessed, have IEPs and reviews, etc. The key worker is the best person to do this. They must use the vocabulary and style of language that the child's familiar with. For example, if the child knows and uses the term 'adult', then you can refer to the outside agents as 'the adults from a different place who come here to help you', but if the child is more familiar with the term 'grown-up', then use those words.

- Similarly, use the same terms when referring to the child's difficulty – take your cue from the phraseology used by the child and their parents/carers; ask them all how they would prefer you to refer to the difficulty, situation, etc. Also remember that the child and their family may not perceive the difficulty as a difficulty, or may perceive it differently from you. Respect this and take it into account – what matters in the end is an effective plan for the child, which will result in an effective outcome for the child!

- Help them to express how they feel about their own difficulties. Talk about their problems and encourage them to say how they feel about it. However, you may be surprised that they have a very positive attitude to the whole situation, which is also an attitude you should strive to project. It's important not to assume it's a 'doom and gloom' scenario, because everybody is working together to support the child, and that's a very positive situation.

- Make sure that the child doesn't focus so much on their difficulties that they think there's nothing else to talk about except their problem. Encourage them to tell you *everything* about themselves, such as their favourite story, film, television programme, toy, game, etc., what makes them laugh or cry, what's their biggest wish, etc. Help them to make a book about themselves, with photos, pictures and what they have said written inside.

- Encourage the child to tell you how they see themselves in the setting. Get them to tell you what they're good at, what they enjoy doing, what they have learned, what they find hard to do, what they don't like doing.

- Help them understand that the things they need help with developing are their additional needs. Use your chosen phrase from the beginning, because the child will hear it a great many times before you've finished the process. Explain that it's the adults' way of describing what things the child needs help with. You can help them understand by talking in terms of the child's particular difficulties.

- Talk about the outside agents and what their part is in the overall plan. Encourage the child to tell you how they feel about this. Get them to draw or photograph the outside agents for the book about themselves.

- If they go on for Statutory Assessment, help them to understand what the process involves. Again, use the correct terminology; explain that it means everybody will be asked to write what things the child is good at, what things they find difficult and what sort of help they need to learn the things they find hard.

- Introduce each member of the team to the child and explain what their job will be. This reassures the child that everybody is working together to make sure the child gets the help they need.

- If a Statement of Special Educational Needs is written, explain to the child that it's just an important paper which has written on it all the things the child needs to help them learn the things they find difficult.

- Prepare the child for any specialised help they may be allocated. Get them to tell you how they feel about this. All of this information will form part of the child's contribution to the Statutory Assessment and/or the Statement.

CD-ROM Resources for this Chapter

Expression of Concern Form

Differentiated Learning Plan

Individual Education Plan

Parent's/Carer's Review Form

Child's Review Form

IEP Review Form

Referral Form to Outside Agent

5

Keeping track – ensuring effective record keeping

> The **key points** covered in this chapter are:
>
> - The crucial importance of setting up and maintaining records.
> - The role of the SENCO regarding records.
> - The different types of records: observations, assessments, examples of work, profiles and checklists, Individual Education Plans (IEPs), IEP/review summaries.
> - Records as evidence.

INTRODUCTION

We live in an age of paper chases and log books, and the special educational needs (SEN) process has records as a fundamental part of its workings. While we may moan and groan about filling in forms and pen pushing, the updating and monitoring of the records of the children in our care are crucial. When we send a child along the path set by the *SEN Code of Practice*, we're talking about a long-term objective, with the development of a young human being at its core. It's that child's entitlement to have their progress and achievements, and their areas of continuing need, recorded and acknowledged over the period of time they're being supported.

SETTING UP AND MAINTAINING RECORDS

You can't over-emphasise the crucial importance of establishing an effective and accurate system of record keeping for children with additional needs. Only by keeping the first observations and expressions of concern, the ongoing records of progress, and the log of final outcomes can the child's achievements be fully appreciated. It's almost like those 'before' and 'after' photos you see in magazines – good records can give an overall picture of how the child has developed and progressed as a result of the support given.

Sometimes a child will make progress in small steps and it's easy to fall into the trap of thinking they're not getting anywhere. Take a look at the first observations, compared with what's happening now, and my guess is you'll see that in fact the child has come a long way from the early days. It's only through keeping accurate records that this picture becomes clear.

Sadly, though, some children don't progress very well, for whatever reason. Again, accurate and objective records are vital for highlighting the child's areas of continuing need. If a child has to move through Early Years Action Plus, and even on to Statutory Assessment, their records will form the main body of evidence required. We'll discuss this in more detail later in the chapter.

As SENCO, you need to make sure that your setting has a record system whereby the practitioners can collect and log information about the child who is causing concern. The system should include:

- various methods of gathering information about and evidence of the child's performance

- a method of expressing concern if their (lack of) progress is worrying

- a system of recording their differentiated curriculum

- clear and effective records of programmes of work, or action plans (e.g. Effective Learning Objectives, Differentiated Learning Plans [DLPs], Individual Education Plans [IEPs], Play Plans, etc. – these are all discussed in greater detail in Chapter 4)

- accurate and practical records of reviews and meetings to monitor the child.

Most settings can access their Local Authority's (LA) record forms, which keep the documentation standardised locally. This helps enormously if a child moves from one setting to another, as their records can go with them. Private and non-maintained settings can design their own forms if they wish to do so, but again it's more practical and sensible to use those that are available from the LA.

The role of the SENCO regarding records

One of your most important roles as SENCO is to make sure that your colleagues maintain the SEN records. Because many of these already form an integral part of the child's profile, and are working documents, this responsibility shouldn't be onerous. Because, too, the *SEN Code of Practice* directs that IEPs or equivalent plans (which are records) are reviewed regularly, they will automatically be updated and monitored.

If you can, establish a 'long-term culture' in your setting, whereby everybody is aware that today's records may be needed to form tomorrow's evidence of action. Later in the chapter, we'll explore the importance of this, since the authorities will ask you to demonstrate *through your records* how you supported the child, and whether you did this effectively. This is particularly important when you go on to Early Years Action Plus, with the involvement of outside agents.

You must also emphasise the necessity of honesty and integrity on the part of everybody who writes the child's records. We saw in Chapter 4 that there's no room for pride in this game, for the child's sake. If a Differentiated Learning Plan (DLP), an IEP or Play Plan isn't addressing the child's needs, the practitioners involved must concede this and re-plan. Time lost for these children is lost forever, and they can't afford for that to happen. Writing records, plans or reviews to present a rosy picture of the child's progress, when in fact the little person is struggling with an action plan that's far too challenging, is unethical and unprofessional. The practitioner who records that they got the planning wrong and are trying again has more professional integrity than one who's economical with the truth in order to appear 'successful'. Sadly, some practitioners will do this, and if this is so in your setting, let it be known that you won't tolerate it. The bottom line is that the child pays the price.

You may have to use all your leadership, diplomatic and communication skills, but you must ensure that good practice is developed in your setting. As with many of these things, by setting an example yourself, you'll be demonstrating good practice to your colleagues. Having 'been there and done it' yourself, you'll be in a strong position to encourage colleagues to follow suit.

If somebody appears to be causing concern in this area, check whether they need some support, training, help or advice. They may be feeling overwhelmed by it all, threatened or afraid of the process. Offering to tackle their concerns will go a long way to preventing long-term difficulties, and this can only be for the children's benefit.

THE DIFFERENT TYPES OF RECORDS AND HOW THESE ARE USED WHEN PLANNING PROGRAMMES FOR THE CHILD

Let's have a look at the commonest ways we have of recording the children's progress.

Observations

Observations are now recognised as the fundamental method of accruing information about a child's performance and progress, and they form an integral part of the Early Years Profile. For decades, early years practitioners have known about the value of observations, but were simultaneously made to feel they were 'wasting time just watching children playing'. Often such comments were made by practitioners who were not early years specialists but held influential or managerial positions within the hierarchy. Thankfully, the UK's governing bodies now acknowledge the tremendous value of observations and have enshrined the practice of using them within the Early Years documents. You should ensure that all practitioners within the setting are familiar with the recommendations made in the Early Years documents regarding observations.

Observations provide a record of what the child can do and you should carry these out in various situations, e.g. play, self-chosen activities, structured activities and adult-led activities. You can then build up an overview of the child's achievements and abilities across the full spectrum of the setting's curriculum.

Observations are also a good way of sharing information about the child with both the parents/carers and other professionals. You can discuss the child with their parents/carers, highlighting your comments from the findings of the observations, so they can see how their child functions in the setting. You can also share the information with other professionals, particularly those who have only just met the child, to help them see the child's full range of abilities.

There are two basic types of observation: the continuous (or narrative) observation and the focused (or targeted) observation.

Continuous (or narrative) observations

Usually all the practitioners in the setting will do these. They comprise short notes jotted down at any time on a day-to-day basis, so forming a record of a child's daily progress and any specific achievements, and helping to build up a picture of their development in the longer term. They briefly record what the child does, together with short, related assessment statements linking up with the relevant targets of the child's curriculum and/or the IEP. The observer(s) should date and initial the form, and put it into the child's profile folder.

Figure 5.1 shows an example of a completed Continuous Observation Form.

There's a blank version of the form on the CD-ROM.

Continuous Observation Form				
Child's name: Una Kelly				
Date of birth: 22.01.05				
Date	**Observation**	**Area of learning**	**Planning**	**Observer**
14.06.09	Una played with a jigsaw – hard to manipulate the pieces	PSD	More activities for fine motor skills, e.g. thread and beads; straws; jigsaws; etc.	C.M.
14.06.09	Una identified her name on three diplays	C L L	Find name in other contexts; identify name card	J.W.
15.06.09	Una destroyed Susan's model and then hit her	PSD	Plan positive behaviour programme	J.W.

Figure 5.1   An example of a completed Continuous Observation Form

Focused (or targeted) observations

Usually only one practitioner in the setting will do these, less frequently and with more of a focus. They will make the observation across a fixed length of time, usually over 10 or 15 minutes, and thereby record what the child does and says. Normally they'd agree with their colleagues when they will do the observation, in order that they can be released from child contact, leading activities or teaching.

All the staff involved with the child should agree how many focused observations should be done per week, per month, half term or term, according to the child's needs. Again, the observer should date and sign the notes.

During the session, the observer can leave out anything the child does that isn't related to the observation focus. So, for example, there isn't any need to write 'Una went to the toilet' if the focus of the observation is to assess Una's early writing skills.

Because of the 'busyness' of early years settings, the observer can make notes with key words and write the observation up properly, either immediately or as soon as possible afterwards.

The observation should be objective and factual to ensure accuracy. The record must state only what happened, not the observer's opinion of what happened. For example, 'Una destroyed Susan's model and then hit her' is more objective and factual than 'Una behaved badly towards Susan'. The first statement tells us exactly what Una did; the second shows us that the observer disapproved of what Una did, but nothing else. 'Behaved badly' is a subjective phrase, meaning different things to different people; it doesn't tell the reader anything relevant about the incident.

When you need to collect information about a child who's causing concern, and where specific evidence of that child's difficulties is needed, focused observations are usually better than continuous observations. It's very important that you repeat an observation if it seems to illustrate a difficulty that the child is experiencing. One session won't give you enough evidence, so you must observe the child at least once more, preferably a couple more times. Ask another practitioner to do an observation to discover whether they can identify the same concerns, but don't share your feelings beforehand so they can maintain their objectivity.

While doing an observation try to be a 'fly on the wall' – that way you can glean objective information. Even if the child does something that requires adult intervention, you must resist the temptation to become involved – leave it to your colleagues to sort out the problem and continue making notes on what's happening. You can then use the information to plan specific targets, strategies and methods to support the child's progress.

Figure 5.2 provides an example of a completed Focused Observation Form.

 There's a blank version of the form on the CD-ROM.

Observations, birth to three

Everything we have discussed so far has been about early years children, but we haven't addressed the issue in relation to babies, from birth to three years. It's just as crucial to keep ongoing observational records about babies as it is for older children – indeed you could argue that it's even more important, since you would be alerted as early as possible if a child wasn't developing as you'd hoped. The Common Assessment Framework is a very useful document for helping to assess how a baby is developing. Filling in the framework can help you focus on which areas of concern need to be addressed. It's also useful to find out whether your LA

Focused Observation Form	
Child's name: Una Kelly	**Date of birth:** 22.01.05
Date and time of observation: 16.06.09; 10.45–11.00	**Observer:** Clare Moore

Una alone at water play, pours water from cup into bowl; mumbling to herself. Goes to sink and fills cup with water, returns to water tray and pours water into watermill. Tries to stop water leaving watermill; gets frustrated ('naughty toy'); leaves water play. Goes to model-making (no place free); stands beside Susan, watches her making model. 'Let me try' – Susan refuses. Una tries to snatch Susan's glue brush; girls tussle and Una slaps Susan's hand; Susan cries and goes to J.W. Una sits on Susan's seat and smashes Susan's model. J.W. intervenes & asks why she hit Susan; Una denies it; J.W. tells Una to leave model-making area. Una goes to Home Corner and plays with doll. Asks to join other children's game; they refuse. Una cuddles doll alone in corner.

<u>Area of learning:</u> Personal and social development

<u>Learning targets:</u>

1. Waiting to take turn if activities not yet available.

2. Being gentle, i.e. controlling urge to hit, etc.

3.

<u>Strategies:</u>

1. Agree system with Una for rewards for each time she waits to take her turn.

2. Plan programme with rewards for specific time-spans spent with specified positive behaviour.

3.

Figure 5.2   An example of a completed Focused Observation Form

and/or *SureStart* team have developed their own recording/observation system which covers the stages from birth onwards. As always, when working with a child who has a disability, a close involvement with their parents/carers will also furnish you with crucial information about that baby's progress. Keep the records accurate and up to date and the baby's portfolio will provide a superb resource for support and ideas, should they be needed later.

Assessments

Our society supports a veritable industry of assessments, starting almost from a child's birth, with charts, records, checklists and so on. While you may feel we've gone totally overboard with it all, be careful not to throw out the baby with the bathwater (no pun intended!) – assessments do have a valuable place in helping us to focus on a child's achievements and areas of need. The skill comes in selecting the appropriate assessment for the particular situation and then in using its results to plan effectively for the child's support. For babies and very young children, I would remind you again of the Common Assessment Framework and its place in assessments.

Speaking very broadly, there are two basic types of assessment: standardised and individualised.

Standardised assessments

These are the commercially-available 'tests' or assessments, produced and validated by official bodies. They will usually become available for use only after much research, careful design and planning, piloting within the target population, a critical analysis of the results, an application of statistics to ensure the results are significant and can be correlated across the target population, and a validation by the appropriate organisations (which can include, for example, government departments, university departments, commercial and private establishments, or any combination of these).

For our purposes, what we're left with, after all of the above, is a test, assessment, checklist, baseline and/or set of criteria that we can use to judge the progress of a child as compared with their national (and sometimes even international) peer group. By applying the assessment, we can see what areas of strength the child has and what skills they need to develop, in relation to other children of their age across the country.

There are pros and cons to standardised assessments, particularly when using them in the early years sector. They can give you an overview of the child's development in a broad sense, but they won't give you a picture of the child's progress in relation to themselves or their recent developmental history. For example, Una may be delayed linguistically for her age, according to a standardised language assessment, but she may have made amazing progress with her language development over the last six months, a fact that won't be reflected in the test (unless it's a repeat of one done earlier in the year – but you need to be wary of 'over-testing' very young children).

If you and your colleagues decide to use a standardised assessment, make sure it's a reliable test, has been validated by a body or organisation with the highest reputation, and is relevant and appropriate to the area of the child's development that you're hoping to measure. Above all, don't use it every five minutes to 'check up' on the child's progress – comparative results are only useful after retests done much later.

Individualised assessments

These are assessments designed with a smaller population in mind and are more 'localised' and specific to the child being assessed. So, for example, any baseline assessments or checklists used by your setting can be classed as individualised because they will measure a child's achievements in relation to their peer group within your setting, within the neighbourhood, and against the child's own development. They can give you a much clearer picture of specific areas of need as well as areas of achievement, thereby helping you to plan for a focus or target which is relevant to a particular child. Most providers now use the EYFS or local equivalent

Profile as their main body of records, but many will add in their own records to give a very full picture of the child's performance and progress.

Your LA may have its own assessments or checklists and these will have been designed with the local population in mind. For example, there wouldn't be much point in trying to assess the language development of a child from an inner London area by using an assessment with vocabulary and concepts based on countryside and rural experiences. Use assessments that are available locally and if you think they need to be adapted to make them a little more appropriate to your situation, you can do this without skewing any results. The beauty of individualised assessments is that they measure the child against themselves, within their own context.

If you're not sure which assessments to use, ask for help in deciding. Your Area SENCO will be able to advise, and your Early Years Learning Support Service (EYLSS) will give you help and information. You could also ask your local educational psychologist (EP) to make some suggestions. But the most important thing is that your choice of assessment is relevant to your children and gives a fair and useful picture of their progress.

Examples of work

Sometimes a child's difficulties will be reflected in their work in the setting. By this I mean the things produced during activities, such as, for example, a painting, some writing, a model, or a photograph you take of them when they're presenting behaviour which illustrates a particular difficulty.

If you feel that something connected with the child or created by the child highlights your concerns, keep it in the child's file. If you need to move to Early Years Action Plus, or even Statutory Assessment, it may prove very important as part of your body of evidence.

 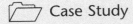 Case Study

Rebecca, aged 4, was displaying some very disturbing behaviour almost every day in the setting. She was being aggressive, both physically and verbally, towards the other children. Practitioners saw her on two occasions performing inappropriate and mature sexual acts on a doll in the Home Corner during solitary play. Eventually the educational psychologist became involved.

One day Rebecca produced a drawing that clearly illustrated male genitalia alongside a female figure. When her key worker asked her what her picture was about she said, 'It's me and Grandad doing our secret'. Rebecca then went on to disclose what seemed to be sexual abuse by her grandfather.

Investigations by child protection officers found this to be the case and Rebecca's grandfather was eventually convicted and jailed. Her picture was used as evidence in drawing up the case for the prosecution (in view of her tender age, she didn't testify in court, but was interviewed by the child protection officers).

The educational psychologist also decided that the abuse was probably at the root of Rebecca's negative behaviour, and indeed after her grandfather was removed from the situation, she became a different child: much happier, relaxed and very social.

Profiles

Every child in an early years setting will have an Early Years Foundation Stage, or local equivalent Profile – a record of their achievements, skills and areas of need – and children with additional needs are no different. Their Profile should show their development and achievements in the six areas of learning of the EYFS:

- Personal, Social and Emotional development (PSE)

- Communication, Language and Literacy (CLL)

- Problem Solving, Reasoning and Numeracy (PSRN)

- Knowledge and Understanding of the World (KUW)

- Physical Development (PD)

- Creative Development (CD).

Practitioners in Northern Ireland, Scotland and Wales will have Profile documents that replicate those of the EYFS, and therefore should use these. There's no need to transfer all the information on a personalised additional needs profile, such as an IEP, to the Profile – you'll only be wasting time duplicating data and the two documents should complement each other anyway – and a note such as 'See IEP', where necessary, should be enough. It's as crucial to keep the Profile up to date as it is the other records. It gives the wider picture of the child's development and should reflect and support the content of the more focused IEP.

Remember, it isn't your job as SENCO to keep a child's records up to date (unless you're their primary practitioner). Your role is to make sure the practitioners working with the child monitor and update the files regularly.

Checklists

The EYFS Profile Scales, or their local equivalent, will be used by early years providers, but some may choose to supplement these with checklists of their own. As always, this is a decision you need to make together as a staff, and in the context of your setting. You can go on forever trying to select a checklist, ranging from commercially-produced versions, to downloaded internet versions, to your own version designed within the setting. Find out what your LA recommends as far as checklists are concerned. Perhaps they've developed their own in order to standardise records across the authority. Which checklists you choose for your setting is entirely up to you, but the choice should be made by everyone. After all, it's they who will be using them, so your colleagues must be comfortable with them.

In relation to a child with additional needs, you might find these questions useful when thinking of drawing up a checklist for your setting. Remember, however, that the following does not in any way constitute a 'diagnosis' or an identification kit. We are educators, not medics, and we work in a multi-disciplinary context in order to identify a child's difficulties. Each section ties in with one of the areas of need as outlined in the *SEN Code of Practice*.

Communication and interaction
Watch for the little one who:

- hardly ever talks or does not talk at all

- stammers or has slow speech, but understands what you say to them, and what they say makes sense

- has delayed or distorted speech that's difficult to understand

- has normal speech but what they say may be odd or inappropriate in context

- has normal speech but doesn't seem to understand what you say to them and/or doesn't respond appropriately to other people

- speaks at inappropriate times or makes inappropriate remarks

- laughs very loudly or for too long

- finds it hard to take turns during conversations and/or has poor conversational skills

- has ritualistic or obsessive behaviours or habits

- has problems communicating through speech and/or other forms of language

- can't use appropriate verbal and/or non-verbal language

- doesn't react 'normally' in social situations or avoids social situations

- behaves passively and has little or no initiative or curiosity

- seems to be unaware of other people and their needs or emotions

- has an unusual voice tone, uses bizarre language and/or ritualistic phrases such as advertisement jingles or slogans.

Cognition and learning
Look out for the child who:

- has poor scores on assessments or profiles compared with other children of the same age in their group

- has markedly lower levels of development (in all or specific areas) and play than those of the other children

- finds difficulty in developing their skills, especially in communication and inter-action, literacy and numeracy

- can't deal with abstract ideas and/or generalise concepts from personal experience (older children)

- makes little or no progress in spite of their involvement in the nursery curriculum

- doesn't achieve their set targets

- makes little or no progress despite your differentiated curriculum.

Behavioural, emotional and social development
Watch for the child who:

- is verbally and/or physically aggressive with other children and/or adults

- is introverted or withdrawn, or seems troubled and worried

- is loud and inappropriately outgoing

- behaves inappropriately for their chronological age

- has strange or socially inappropriate behaviour

- does things that may cause self-injury

- can't stay on task, despite support and encouragement from an adult

- regularly disrupts the routine

- doesn't make progress

- is often absent

- has bouts of uncooperative behaviour

- behaves unpredictably and/or has erratic attitudes to learning

- shows little interest in activities and games

- seems to be over-dependent on adults

- seems to be hyperactive

- either can't play with other children, or play with them 'normally'

- can't share or take turns with toys and equipment

- shows poor or no conversational skills.

Sensory and/or physical
See if the child:

- has difficulty in coordinating their hands and feet

- experiences problems in balancing

- has poor gross and/or fine motor skills

- moves around clumsily.

They may have visual difficulties if they:

- hold books and objects close to their face to look at them

- always sit at the front for stories or television and then strain to look at the book or TV

- bang into or trip over objects

- have a lack of confidence when moving around the room and/or show anxiety about banging into things

- find difficulty in focusing on an object or have problems in eye tracking

- have difficulty in doing activities that require visual skills and/or have difficulty with hand–eye coordination

- have unusual eye movements such as roving or 'trembling' of the eyeball

- display abnormal social interaction or autistic-type behaviours

- hold their head in an unusual position

- display eye poking, rocking or other 'blindisms'

They may have hearing difficulties if they:

- concentrate intensively on the faces and body gestures of the adults in the setting

- either don't follow instructions, follow instructions only sometimes and/or follow instructions wrongly

- don't respond to their name, especially if you call them from behind

- watch the other children before doing an action, and then copy the others

- appear to need more visual input and support during activities than other children in the group

- behave inappropriately or seem to be frustrated without any apparent cause

- don't react to loud or unexpected noises

- shout or talk too loudly without realising it

- have delayed speech or speech that's difficult to understand

- change their voice tone while they're speaking

- have difficulty doing activities that require listening skills

- have discharges from their ear(s), which don't seem to clear up or which occur quite frequently

- tilt their head when listening to stories, instructions, and so on

- appear to be in a world of their own or showing autistic-type behaviours.

These checklists are not to be interpreted as a 'diagnosis' or a way of labelling a child. Use them only to give yourself an indication of which areas of development you might need to focus on to support the child most effectively.

If you are drawing up a checklist for babies, you may find it helpful to look at the section 'Helping to identify children with additional needs' on the CD-ROM (Chapter 3).

Individual Education Plans (IEPs)

IEPs are explored in greater detail in Chapter 4. (Remember that you may decide to use Effective Learning Objectives, Individualised Learning Programme, or another form of tailor-made action plan. Whatever your chosen system, it will be the same in principle as an IEP.) Here we will just have a quick reminder of the acronym that characterises the targets of IEPs:

SMART:

- Specific – written concisely so everybody knows exactly what the child's aims are

- Measurable – so everybody knows exactly when these aims have been achieved

- Achievable – so everybody knows the targets can be reached and how the child will do this

- Recorded – so everybody knows the progress being made

- Time-defined – so everybody knows by when (i.e. the date) the targets should be achieved.

Let's have a look at the example IEP from Chapter 4 in terms of SMART (see Figure 5.3).

Notice that Harry's targets are written in *Specific* terms, making his aims quite clear. The criteria for success outline exactly how his achievements will be *Measurable*. The targets are *Achievable* because they've been chosen as the next stage from Harry's current strengths. The information *Recorded* on the IEP form satisfies this requirement. The 'deadline' date shows that Harry's targets are *Time-defined*.

The IEPs are probably your most important records and getting them right is crucial. The reason for this is discussed in the section *Records as evidence* below.

IEP/review summaries

To save you rummaging through every child's file to jog your memory about what stage they've reached, you could have a Summary Sheet similar to the one shown in Figure 5.4.

Individual Education Plan	
Child's name: Harry Jones	**DOB:** 29.03.04
Date IEP implemented: 13.01.09	**Code of Practice level:** E Y Action

Areas of strength: Harry enjoys books; he paints excellent pictures.
Areas of difficulty: Harry has difficulty with early number work. He has hearing problems – he's got grommets; he regularly attends the ear nose & throat department at the hospital.
Targets to be reached by: 8.04.09
1) Harry will be able to count from 1 to 4 using apparatus.
2) Harry will be able to recognise and name 1 to 4 when shown in written form.
3) Harry will be able to write any numeral from 1 to 4 on request.
Criteria for success:
1) Harry will count from 1 to 4 using four different types of apparatus, 4 times out of 5.
2) Harry will recognise and name 1, 2 ,3 or 4 in written form in a variety of places, 4 times out of 5.
3) Harry will correctly write a requested numeral from 1 to 4, 4 times out of 5.
Teaching methods: initially in a one-to-one situation in the quiet area; then in the main nursery areas to use counting displays, posters, name tags, etc.
Staff involved: Mrs Smith, early years teacher; Mrs Scott, nursery nurse; Mrs Jones, mother, to work at home.
Frequency of programme: twice daily (morning and afternoon) for a maximum of ten minutes, five days per week; once per evening at home when possible.
Equipment/Apparatus: cubes, counters, plastic sorting shapes, any appropriate counting apparatus of Harry's choice, paper, pencils and felt-tip pens.
Date of next review: 9.04.09
To be attended by Mrs Smith, Mrs Scott & Mrs Jones.

Figure 5.3   Making an IEP SMART

This is a quick reference as to what's happening over any three-monthly/termly period. Make sure that it's:

- accessible to all staff

- displayed somewhere private and confidential

- updated regularly – pop the dates and data on straight after each review.

IEP/Review Summary Sheet

Summary Year: 2009

1 Jan–31 March 2009				
Child's name	Code of Practice level	IEP no. & date implemented	Last review date & outcome	Next review due
Harry Jones	EY Action	No. 1: 13.01.09	Not applicable yet	9.04.09
John Davies	EY Action Plus	No. 3: 12.12.08	11.12.08 Move to EYA+	21.03.09
Sadie Scott	EY Action Plus	No. 3: 10.12.08	21.03.09 Refer for Statutory Assessment	1.06.09
1 April–30 June 2009				
1 July–30 September 2009				
1 October–31 December 2009				

Figure 5.4   Example of a completed IEP/Review Summary Sheet

RECORDS AS EVIDENCE

The value placed on the records of a child with additional needs can't be rated too highly. They're not just another set of files from which the authorities can draw statistics for the government returns. They're the hard evidence of a child's achievements, development and continuing areas of need. It's vital that everyone in your setting places great store by these records, not least because they may be your key to accessing further support for the child should they need it.

You might now be thinking, *What's this woman talking about?* It's very simple. If a child moves on to Early Years Action Plus and/or Statutory Assessment, their records will form the basis on which decisions will be made that will affect provision for the child. It's clear from this how crucially important it is to have accurate and continuous records. So let's see what I *am* talking about!

Early years action plus

As we've already seen, this is the level of the *SEN Code of Practice* where you will ask for the help and advice of an outside agent. Remember, it's possible (even likely) that the agent won't know your little one from Adam. They will have to rely on the information you give them to build up a picture of that child's achievements and difficulties. It could have taken anything up to a year for you to reach this stage, so an accurate record of what was happening a year ago, in the interim, and also very recently, will be needed. Suppose the child is 4 years old. If it has taken one year to reach the Early Years Action Plus, that's a quarter of their entire lifespan – quite a daunting thought. The agent's support (type, level, quantity, etc.) will be influenced by what's in your records, so make them good ones!

Statutory Assessment

If the child moves to Statutory Assessment, the LA's going to ask you for all the child's records. But, crucially, they're going to ask you to show:

- whether you consulted outside agents

- whether you took the advice of the outside agents

- how you implemented that advice

- what form the liaison between yourselves and the outside agents took.

If you present the LA with faulty, 'spotty', inaccurate and/or incomplete records, they may decide there's insufficient evidence of SEN. You'll have poured down the drain in one go, all the time, effort, and commitment, and, what's worse, you may delay the child's entitlements being met. This isn't a melodramatic view – it's what can happen through poor administration. We owe it to the children not to let that happen.

CD-ROM Resources for this Chapter

Continuous Observation Form

Focused Observation Form

Making an IEP SMART: a completed IEP form

IEP/Review Summary Sheet

Case study REBECCA (Chapter 5)

Helping to Identify Children with Additional Needs 1–15 (Chapter 3)

6

A parent thing – maintaining a collaborative partnership

> The **key points** covered in this chapter are:
> - Involving the parents/carers at various levels.
> - Designing and using Play Plans.
> - Parent Partnership Services.
> - Parents/carers with differing needs.
> - Documentation for parents/carers.

INTRODUCTION

Here we'll look at your role in ensuring that the parents/carers are supported at all levels of involvement in the special educational needs (SEN) process. We'll explore your duties with regard to Parent Partnership Services (PPS) and also the issues involved when the parents/carers themselves have additional needs, and how you can ensure that they're included in the process, despite their difficulties.

INVOLVING THE PARENTS/CARERS

Parents/carers of children with additional needs have the right to become involved from your earliest concerns onwards and, as SENCO, you have a major responsibility to ensure this happens. Indeed, this is at the core of the Early Years Foundation Stage framework, or local equivalents, and is a non-negotiable right of the parents/carers (and of the child!).

There are various degrees of involvement by parents/carers, depending on which level of the *SEN Code of Practice* we're talking about. This can include, for example:

- having a quick word at pick-up time about the day's events

- keeping a home/setting diary (daily or weekly)

- collaborating on Play Plans

- sharing Individual Education Plans (IEPs) or an equivalent action plan

- discussing the way forward via reviews.

SOME PRACTICALITIES OF PARENTAL/CARER INVOLVEMENT

- If the child's difficulties have only recently been identified, the parents/carers might be going through a grieving process, so be sensitive to their feelings. If you're supporting a baby whose problem was identified at birth, for example, Down's Syndrome or cerebral palsy, you will need to be supportive of and empathetic towards the parents/carers, because they may still be trying to adjust to a situation that's different from the one they expected. If the child is older and the difficulty has only recently been recognised, it's possible and/or probable that the parents/ carers will still be going through the adjustment stage and will need your support.

- Be prepared for a variety of reactions: disbelief, denial, grief, self-blame, even aggression. There may also be 'Thank goodness, someone's believed me and given it a name!' There can, in addition, be over-protection and extreme anxiety. Understand and make allowances for any of these.

- Bear in mind that parents/carers may perceive an additional need/disability in a different way from the way you do. For example, they may not consider deafness as a disability or impairment, and would therefore not refer to the child as being 'hearing impaired'. Take your cue from them, and use the same terminology as they do. It's also very important that you never refer to a child as 'suffering from …', even if (arguably, especially if!) their difficulty is medical-based. The child with a difficulty or condition *has* x, y, or z – but they are highly unlikely to be 'suffering' from it.

- Listen to the parents/carers, giving them time to talk, but do use this approach wisely – you and the other children also have needs, so make sure these are met too.

- Give the parents/carers encouragement and positive feedback about their child's progress, efforts, positive behaviour and achieved targets. They will need something positive to hang on to – even something like 'Laura's tried very hard today, Mrs Jones – we're really pleased with her.'

- Don't tell them that the child has achieved something unless they really have – it's vitally important to be truthful.

- Always tell parents/carers about any discussions that have taken place if an outside agent has 'popped in' to talk to you and the parents/carers weren't present.

- Without being patronising, give them credit for any support or follow-up work they do at home. You'll reduce their sense of isolation and they'll know that they're *doing* something for their child and doing it well.

- Be a mutual support group. The parents/carers will know how their child reacts to things at home; you will know how they react in the setting. Sharing this information will give all of you a resource of knowledge about the child that you can use in your planning.

- When they're ready for it, give the parents/carers the contact details of relevant societies, associations, self-help groups, etc., which can provide another strand of support that they may welcome. Be extremely careful to recommend only the long-established and *bona fide* organisations, however. This is particularly important when the parents/carers begin to search for information on the internet. Advise them of the value of reading information that comes from the websites of only recognised and validated organisations.

- Ask them everything you want to know about their child. They're the experts and can be a fount of information that you can exploit. Never discuss their child in an inappropriate place or manner, or with an inappropriate person.

- If the parents/carers are following a Play Plan or home-based programme, emphasise that as soon as the child shows any boredom, distraction or distress, they should stop doing the activity. If the child is forced to continue, they won't enjoy the activity, therefore they won't gain anything from it and they may even turn against it, thereby defeating your whole aim.

- If the parents/carers aren't familiar with the songs, rhymes and games you use in the setting, invite them to sit in on a few sessions at drop-off or collection time. They will very quickly pick up the technique.

ACTIVITY REPORTS

Encourage the child's key worker to set up a home/setting activity report to tell the parents/carers about:

- the child's current target

- the games and activities being used to achieve the target

- the child's progress towards achieving the target (in positive terms, e.g. 'Andrew can identify his name card from among five others', not 'Andrew still can't say what sound his name begins with')

- how the child keeps their own records (e.g. Andrew might have his own book of stickers or a chart with balloons to colour in).

Decide between yourselves how often to send the report back and forth. Some settings will choose to use a daily report, others will do it on a weekly basis. Figure 6.1 shows an example of a completed Weekly Activity Report. Depending on the child's achievement level, you can help them complete the form, or fill it in for them, writing what they tell you.

There's a blank version of the form on the CD-ROM. You can easily adapt it to a Daily Activity Report, and change it in other ways to suit your particular needs (or perhaps your LA has its own *pro forma*).

Weekly Activity Report
My name is Andrew Johnson
Today is Friday 13 March 2009
I'm trying to fasten my coat buttons all by myself **and** listen to stories quietly
This week I played with the button-fastening game, the dressing up box, the teddies **and** the books in the story corner, the computer and the stories on the tape recorder
Now I can fasten 2 buttons on my coat **and** listen quietly for three minutes
This week I filled in five balloons on my clown chart

Figure 6.1   An example of a completed Weekly Activity Report

PLAY PLANS

A Play Plan is a very effective method of involving the parents/carers in doing support and follow-up work with the child at home. The targets of a Play Plan are linked with those of the child's Effective Learning Objectives (ELOs), Differentiated Learning Plan (DLP) or IEP, and incorporate games, activities and play sessions that will reinforce your teaching points. It's a good way of sharing information about the child's progress and also lets the child see that you and their parents/carers are working together to support them. Play Plans are also often referred to as Individual Plans or IPs.

 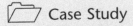 Case Study

Cindy has Down's Syndrome and some accompanying learning difficulties. She's learning her colours, particularly red and green (other colours will be added later). Her mum and the early years practitioner developed a Play Plan aimed at getting Cindy to recognise and name the two colours correctly whenever she is asked. The first part of the Play Plan states what Cindy's targets are and how her mum will help her work towards them. The second section is for Cindy's mum to make a record of her progress. Figure 6.2 shows the completed Play Plan.

Play Plan for <u>Cindy Davis </u>and <u>Cindy's Mum </u>
<u>Cindy </u>will play these games to help <u>Cindy to recognise red and green and to say their names:</u>
Sorting and naming all the red things she can find, followed by green things when she knows red very well.
Painting and potato printing using red first, then green when she knows red.

Sorting and matching all the red shapes, then the green ones.
Naming red things that she takes out of the feely bag; then the green ones.

<u>Begin by</u>
looking at lots of red things (never mind about green at first); help Cindy to sort out all her red clothes (socks, jumpers, hat, etc.); say the word 'red' each time and encourage Cindy to repeat it. Then ask 'What colour is this?' – if Cindy needs to be reminded, say 'red' again.
Here's what <u>Cindy</u> **did:**

Tuesday 4 May. Cindy seemed to mix up the colour with the clothes at first – she'd say Sock when I asked what colour it was, but then she'd say Red after I said it.

Wednesday 5 May. Cindy spotted her dad's red rugby shirt and shouted Red.

Thursday 6 May. We started looking at green today. She seems to be getting the hang of it. She pointed to my mug and said Green. Her older sister's helping her too.

Saturday 8 May. Cindy can tell you red or green almost every time you ask, no matter what you point to. I think she's ready to move on to the next colours.

Date when this Play Plan was finished at home: <u>Sunday 9 May</u>

Figure 6.2   An example of a completed Play Plan for home/setting liaison

There's a blank Play Plan Form on the CD-ROM. You can adapt it to suit your own requirements or use it as it stands.

PARENT PARTNERSHIP SERVICES

All Local Authorities (LAs) have a legal obligation to make arrangements for a Parent Partnership Service (PPS), with the aim of ensuring that the parents/carers of a child with additional needs will receive the support, advice, help and information that they're entitled to. The LA doesn't have to provide the PPS themselves – they may prefer to commission outside providers to offer the service and this is perfectly acceptable. Their obligation is to ensure the parents/carers can access the service easily. When they establish the PPS, they should make arrangements for the involvement of the voluntary sector and organisations, which can advise about specific areas of need and give relevant and appropriate support to the parents/carers.

As SENCO, it's one of your duties to tell the child's parents/carers about the PPS, what it offers and how they can access it. Your LA should have provided you with all the paperwork, information, leaflets and brochures, contact details, etc., that you need. If you don't have this documentation, contact the SEN department of your education offices and ask for everything they have about their PPS. Alternatively, ask your Area SENCO where you can access the information. Usually, *SureStart* centres will have copies of all the relevant literature too.

The main function of the PPS is to help, advise and support the parents/carers of children with additional needs. This includes liaison between parents/carers and practitioners if there are difficulties between home and the setting. By handling such situations sensitively, the PPS can help prevent difficulties from developing into disagreements.

The *SEN Code of Practice* outlines the minimum standards that the PPS should meet. As SENCO, you'll be in a strong position if you're aware of these standards, since you can check that your LA does indeed support your parents/carers through its PPS. The standards are as follows:

- The provision of a range of flexible services including their best endeavours to provide access to an Independent Parental Supporter for all parents who want one.

- That practical support is offered to parents, either individually or in groups, to help them in their discussions with schools, LAs and other statutory agencies.

- That parents (including all those with parental responsibility for the child) are provided with accurate, neutral information on their rights, roles and responsibilities within the SEN process, and on the wide range of options that are available for their children's education.

- That parents are informed about other agencies, such as health services, social services and voluntary organisations, which can offer information and advice about their child's particular SEN. This may be particularly important at the time the LA issues a proposed statement.

- That, where appropriate and in conjunction with their parents, the ascertainable views and wishes of the child are sought and taken into consideration.

- That information about the available services is published widely in the area using a variety of means.

- The provision of neutral, accurate information for parents on all SEN procedures as set out in SEN legislation and the *SEN Code of Practice*.

- The interpretation of information published by schools, LAs and other bodies interested in SEN.

- That a wide range of information for parents is available in community languages, and to parents who may not be able to gain access to information through conventional means.

- That advice on special educational needs procedures is made available to parents through information, support and training.

- They use their best endeavours to recruit sufficient Independent Parental Supporters to meet the needs of parents in their area, including arrangements for appropriate training, ensuring that they are kept up to date with all relevant aspects of SEN policy and procedures so that they can fulfil their role effectively.

- That training on good communication and relationships with parents is made available to teachers, governors and staff in SEN sections of the LA.

- They work with schools, LA officers, and other agencies to help them develop positive relationships with parents.

- They establish and maintain links with voluntary organisations.

- That parents' views are heard and understood, and can inform and influence the development of local SEN policy and practice.

- The regular review of the effectiveness of the service they provide, for instance by seeking feedback from users.

(*Special Educational Needs Code of Practice*, DfES, 2001: 2:21)

You'll find some useful website addresses at the end of this chapter.

PARENTS/CARERS WITH DIFFERING NEEDS

Some parents/carers of children with additional needs may have additional needs themselves. In this case, you must make sure that your cooperation and support are sensitive, understanding and respectful. Bear in mind that they may have had unhappy educational experiences as children themselves and could be feeling extremely threatened by the situation they find themselves in. They may be anxious that their child is going to come up against the same negative attitudes that they themselves did. As SENCO, you must do everything you can to reassure them. Let them see how times have changed by adopting a positive, warm and supportive approach, and by encouraging their involvement in an appropriate way.

You need to be aware of and sensitive to the parents'/carers' perspective of the situation, which could be very different from yours, simply because of their differing needs. It's essential that you work together to find common ground for making sure the child receives the support and help they're entitled to from the home/setting collaboration. Try to see things from the parents'/carers' point of view and go forward from that position.

However, it's also important never to make assumptions about the parents'/carers' perceptions of their child's difficulties. Never assume that they're living the 'worst case scenario' – indeed they may not see the child's disability as a disability or a problem. If they surprise you by maintaining a positive attitude and approach, perhaps you need to re-examine your own perception of the situation, and adopt a more positive stance yourself! What I call the 'Oh dear, what a shame' syndrome is still worryingly evident and if you're aware of any practitioners in your setting suffering from this (and yes, I do mean 'suffering' from it!), try your best to promote the kinds of positive attitudes and actions that are so vital for helping the child to progress.

Parents'/carers' own differing needs can be varied – for example, learning difficulties, a disability, communication or linguistic difficulties, social difficulties and even political challenges which affect their daily lives. These needs should be respected, and you must make sure that the parents/carers receive the same standard of courtesy and support as all the parents/carers do. If, for example, they'd like to bring another family member to meetings to help and support them, then you should be very willing for this to happen (I've even experienced a mother's MP being present at a meeting!); if they'd like to have the support of a translator, whether in another language or in another system of communication for the same reasons, then, once again, be flexible enough to welcome this.

Parents/carers with additional needs may find it difficult to attend your meetings because of commitments connected with their own needs. For example, a parent with a long-term medical condition may have to attend hospital appointments during your allocated review times. You should try to be flexible in situations like this and offer alternative appointments, tying in where you can with the parents'/carers' commitments.

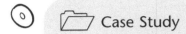

Case Study

Marian's son Billy is four and attends his local nursery, aiming to transfer to the infant school next term. Billy is a hearing child and he is working on an Effective Learning Plan that's targeting his language and communication skills. Marian is profoundly deaf and communicates by using British Sign Language (BSL). At IEP planning sessions and IEP reviews, Marian needs the help of a signing interpreter. By coincidence, the head of the nursery is a qualified and experienced teacher of the deaf, who uses BSL proficiently. She joins the members of Billy's team at their meetings to provide the interpretation that Marian and the others need, to communicate effectively.

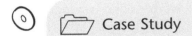

Case Study

Jade's mum, Louise, has learning difficulties and attended a (segregated) special school herself. Fortunately, her school career was very happy and she doesn't have any reservations about Jade going through the SEN process. Jade also has learning difficulties and, at six, is working well in the Early Years Foundation Stage. Louise sometimes finds it hard to understand the finer details of the planning and decision-making for Jade, so comes to the meetings and reviews with her own mum, Barbara. Together they take a full and active part in planning Jade's IEPs, and Barbara helps with the home sessions as well.

The societal and demographic structures in Britain are undergoing change very quickly and many settings are now admitting children from non-indigenous and very varied cultural backgrounds. Some families have arrived in the UK as a result of conflict in their own country and may possibly be experiencing trauma as a consequence. Others may have immigrated for economic and/or social reasons, and may need help and support in adapting to and settling into the system here. Yet others are here for educational reasons; for example, with the child's parents attending university before planning to return to their home country after graduating. Whatever the reason for a family's residence in Britain, if they have a child with additional needs, we have a duty of care to that child and their family in the same way as we have to all children.

As practitioners, we need to be aware of and empathetic with the circumstances of the family, and if necessary review our opinions, approaches and attitudes to make sure we support a child appropriately. This may make for some uncomfortable soul-searching but it is vital if we are to maintain our professional integrity and rise above political and/or social prejudices, in order to ensure each child's development.

RECORDS AND DOCUMENTATION

In earlier chapters, we've seen some examples of record keeping and documentation that could form part of the child's folio. All documentation regarding the child should be clear, concise and easy to understand, and, above all, freely available to the parents/carers. Let them know that you're willing to talk them through the documentation about their child. They must feel relaxed and comfortable enough to ask you to explain anything they don't understand.

Most parents/carers are keen and positive about becoming involved in their child's programmes and action plans. If they perhaps lack a little confidence about becoming involved and/or their ability to support their child, let them see from the Play Plans, IEPs and other records that we're not talking about anything complicated. These are all good, down-to-earth, practical tactics, shared and tried until the 'magic formula' is discovered – the key to giving their child that starting point to achievement.

Some parents/carers, however, may choose not to become involved with the work you're doing with their child, and in that case you must make sure that the child's support is rock solid within the setting. This choice on the part of the parents/carers doesn't mean that you can ignore them, or that you don't need to keep them updated about their child's progress. Through letters, reports and, where possible, personal contact, you should continue to inform them of how you're helping their child.

On the CD-ROM there are some examples of letters you can send to parents/carers who, for whatever reason, haven't kept in touch with you, haven't attended contact sessions/meetings or haven't become involved with their child's programmes. As always, these letters are only examples, but you can use them as a framework to formulate your own in a style and language more appropriate for your parents/carers.

Always make copies of any letters and documentation you send home, particularly if the child's parents/carers are uncooperative or uninvolved, and keep these in the child's file. Also, send your letters and documents by post, getting proof of posting. Sadly, you may have to prove at some stage that you did indeed try to keep the parents/carers closely involved with what you were doing, and these copies and proof of posting may be your only 'evidence'.

Early years action plus

If you decided at the review that the child should move to Early Years Action Plus, it's imperative that you inform their parents/carers immediately – don't refer the child to any outside agent until you've spoken to the parents/carers. If the parents/carers are very difficult to contact, don't battle along on your own any longer. GET ADVICE! There are various options you can take, depending on the child's circumstances.

- Contact your Area SENCO/Inclusion Officer and discuss how to find a way forward.

- Speak to the PPS, respecting the parents'/carers' confidentiality, and ask their advice. They should be able to offer you some practical suggestions.

- If a social worker is involved with the family, you could ask them to speak to the parents/carers about the potential referral to an outside agent.

- The health visitor may be willing to pay a visit and try to persuade the parents/carers to become involved, or at least give you permission to refer. Don't speak to them, however, unless they're already involved with the family – bringing them in 'cold' goes against the spirit of the *SEN Code of Practice*.

- Is there a practitioner in the setting who's closer to the parents/carers and who they might be more willing to speak to? Is there a practitioner who is from the same cultural background and who could help?

- Is only one parent resisting your invitations? Perhaps the other parent can become involved and be able to offer support.

At the end of the day, you will still need to have the willing cooperation and support of the child's parents/carers, so try to keep the situation as positive and amicable as possible. Calling in 'the heavy mob' may indeed succeed in forcing the parents/carers to face the situation, but then what? You're certainly not going to have a pleasant working relationship afterwards. Try to meet them on their terms – remember they may be very frightened, very threatened, even fearful that you're going to take their child away from them – and keep reassuring them that you're on their side. The ultimate goal for all of you is the child's progress, welfare and development; you're batting on the same team, so be persistent in your support of the parents/carers, too, and hopefully it will all come right in the end.

CD-ROM Resources for this chapter

Weekly Activity Report

Case study CINDY (Chapter 6)

Play Plan

Case study BILLY (Chapter 6)

Case study JADE (Chapter 6)

Letters to Difficult-to-Reach Parents/Carers

Useful websites

Parents' Centre – information and support for parents on how to help with their child's learning, including advice on choosing a school and finding childcare:
http://www.parentscentre.gov.uk/educationandlearning/specialneeds/

Contact a Family – the only UK-wide charity providing advice, information and support to the parents of all disabled children.
http://www.cafamily.org.uk/

Family Action – the UK's leading family charity, tackling some of the most complex and difficult issues facing families today
http://www.family-action.org.uk/

National Parent Partnership Network
www.parentpartnership.org.uk

The National Academy for Parenting Practitioners
http://www.parentingacademy.org/

7

Coming together – the teamwork approach

> The **key points** covered in this chapter are:
>
> - The rationale behind the referral.
> - The why, who, and what of outside agency involvement.
> - The child – the central character in the referral.

INTRODUCTION

The original plans didn't work; the child's still causing concern; it's time to take further action – Early Years Action Plus, characterised by requesting outside agents to share with you their more specialised knowledge and experience. Here we'll have a look at the process in more detail.

THE RATIONALE BEHIND THE REFERRAL

There's no need for anxiety, either by you as SENCO or by your colleagues, when you reach the point of referring a child to an outside agent. It's the next logical step in the graduated approach of supporting the child. So what's it all about? Let's explore the reasons.

THE WHY, WHO, AND WHAT OF OUTSIDE AGENCY INVOLVEMENT

Why involve outside agents?

Don't know why you've been sent here – we don't have special needs in this school. Worked here for thirty years and never needed help yet.

These were the words I was greeted with on my first visit to a tiny primary school in the Yorkshire Dales, in 1987. The whole concept of the teamwork approach was new and very daunting to many professionals. This comment was made by a head teacher whose practices had never before been questioned, and who felt very threatened by the 'slip of a lass' (as I was then!) who had been sent to her school to support a child with recognised needs. Hopefully we've come a long way from those days, and practitioners in training now learn from the outset the value and necessity of working as a team.

That head teacher's professional self-esteem was low. She felt de-skilled, unsuccessful and challenged. Sadly, there are still practitioners who will perceive a decision to ask for outside help as a negative judgement on their professionalism, that somehow they've 'failed' to support a child. As SENCO, you will play a crucial role in ensuring your colleagues don't develop these unhelpful feelings and perceptions. In fact, it's arguable that being able to claim on your CV that you have experience of working successfully in a multi-disciplinary team situation will add strength to your professional attractiveness!

You will usually call in an outside agent to support a child because they have more specialised experience, skills and expertise in specific areas of the child's development than can be offered by the practitioners in your setting. This isn't to say that the experience and expertise within your setting are of less value – far from it. As professionals, you and your colleagues will have wide-ranging expertise in mainstream early years practice. It's important to acknowledge this and recognise the immense value it has in the successful planning for and support of the child with additional needs. You will also have an overview of the usual stages of child development, and are therefore in a superb position to identify a child who doesn't pass these at an appropriate time, or in an appropriate way. It's this information about the child, based on your knowledge and expertise, that you will hand over to the outside agent.

We can use an analogy here of a joiner and a cabinet-maker: both can create beautiful things with wood using similar skills; if you needed a staircase, you'd probably ask the joiner; if you needed intricately carved spindles on it, you'd ask the cabinetmaker. Neither craftsman is 'better' than the other – their expertise is simply different. It's the same with our profession. Seen in this context, it's crucial that we peel back any false pride we may have, and overcome any feelings of inadequacy or threat. We must realise the implications for the child of not calling in an outside agent when one is needed. We must also have the integrity to accept our professional limitations and ask for help.

You'll find more details about how you actually ask for this help, how you refer a child to an outside agent, on page 47.

Who are the outside agents?

In Chapter 4 (see page 45) there's a sort of 'Who's Who' of outside agents, the external professionals you'd be most likely to ask for help. Figure 7.1 summarises this. The *Special Educational Needs (SEN) Code of Practice* gives four important principles for a successful inter-agency partnership:

- early identification

- continual engagement with the child and parents/carers

- focused intervention

- dissemination of effective approaches and techniques.

Early identification

It's unarguable that early identification of any difficulty is crucial, particularly when talking about early years children with additional needs. For this reason, you're in the front line when it comes to spotting a child whose progress is causing concern. Even if you can't identify the specific difficulty, you will know from the child's performance relative to the rest of their peer group that there's something you need to investigate, and you're in the best position to call for specialised help early on. Time wasted is the child's time lost, so the sooner specialised help is put in place, the better.

Case Study

Jane, who is 17 months old, was born with severe brain damage after a traumatic and lengthy labour. The *SureStart* team, which includes health, education and social service professionals, have coordinated their involvement, and are working with Jane's parents to follow the Early Start programme. It was decided that the Portage scheme was the most effective way forward, and Jane's parents now receive weekly visits from the physiotherapist, who teaches them what to do. The health visitor and the social worker are also working with Jane's parents, assessing their needs as well as Jane's. Because there are two other small children in the family, both with their own demands on their parents' time and energy, life can become fraught. The social worker has arranged one weekend a month of respite care for Jane, to enable her parents to spend time together with her brothers. The respite carer, who happens to be a Learning Support Assistant at the local school for children with special needs, became Jane's key worker when Jane joined the school's nursery after her mother's maternity leave had finished. This is an excellent example of good practice in action.

Continual engagement with the child and parents/carers

The first twenty-five years of integration/inclusion of children with additional needs have shown the enormous benefits of working closely with the parents/carers and the child. In the early days, I think it's fair to say, parental involvement was often the good practice of an inspired professional rather than a requirement or legislation, but it's now regarded as the norm. The benefits shared by everyone in the team, from the child to the outside agent, include:

- a feeling of belonging

- a sense of empowerment

- possession of the facts

- openness of information

- sharing of a commitment

- reduction of anxieties

- pooling of ideas and suggestions

- confidence in knowing what to do and when

- because of joint support willingness to rewrite a failing plan.

The biggest beneficiary is the child – the reason why we're all part of this in the first place!

Focused intervention

While you will have the experience and expertise gained from an overview of the wider early years picture, you may feel less confident in your knowledge of a specialised field. Even practitioners with a special needs qualification are likely to have studied only one particular field of difficulty, for example, learning difficulties or communication and language problems, and so will still benefit from cooperating with those outside agents who are specialists in other areas. Asking for support from an outside agent helps to sharpen up your approaches to, and perceptions of, a child's difficulties. It allows you to focus more specifically on methods and strategies that are likely to be effective and have a positive outcome for a child's learning and development.

 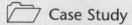 Case Study

> Andrew, aged four years, moved house and started at the nearby nursery. Within a few minutes he had begun to behave inappropriately, being extremely aggressive towards the other children and physically assaulting them. Sometimes there was no apparent reason for his attacks. He couldn't concentrate on an activity for longer than a minute, and he skipped from one to another without completing any of them. The staff and Andrew's mother (Dad had left the family eight months previously) planned and put into place an IEP aimed at helping Andrew to develop positive behaviour and increase his concentration. But the episodes of Andrew's aggression towards the other children increased and some of the other parents/carers complained about his behaviour. Everyone attended an early review meeting and decided to refer Andrew to the educational psychologist and the pre-school behaviour support service.

Dissemination of effective approaches and techniques

Something learned is never wasted and you'll find that, having used a specialised method with one child, you will become more confident in trying similar techniques with another child who is having difficulties. There's never any guarantee that the same technique will succeed with two different children, but when you work closely with an outside agent, you'll feel better about asking for, trying out, and expanding on many more ways around a problem. This is much more effective than attempting to go forward unsupported – remember, if you don't know the answer, you *must* ask somebody who does, for the child's sake.

These approaches and techniques should be child-centred and flexible, and Figure 7.1 highlights how this is the case, with the child at the nucleus of any planning. All

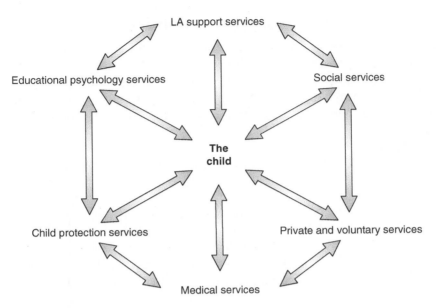

Figure 7.1 Support using a child-centred approach

agencies must, of course, have a system of close liaison with everybody else in the team, ensuring the interchange of ideas and information.

To save you a bit of time, it's useful to have a quick-reference register as to which outside agents are supporting which children. It always happens that when you need to phone somebody in a hurry, and you can't find the number, you end up wading through the filing cabinet or the LA directory, trying to locate the information you want. Having a pro forma such as Figure 7.2, an example of a completed Outside Agency Summary Form, ensures that the vital statistics are instantly to hand. Like all such documentation, however, make sure it's kept somewhere out of general view.

There is a blank version of this form on the CD-ROM.

Child's name & DOB	Outside agent(s)	Agency	Contact details
Christina Simpson 14.03.06	David Johns	Ed. Psych	Tel. 02341 456739
Manjit Kaur 31.10.08	Ann Lowe	E. Years Support	Tel. 02341 567390
	Mandy Smith	Speech & Lang. Therapist	Tel. 02341 927395
Jacob Nathanson 25.03.07	Dan Scott	Behaviour Support	Tel. 02341 453923

Figure 7.2 An example of a completed Outside Agency Summary Form

What would be the outside agents' involvement?

I can't give you the answer to this question! It very much depends on such things as the nature and severity of the child's difficulty, the resources available in your locality, the workload of the outside agents you call in, to name just a few variables. But, by the following general exploration of the type of involvement that you're most likely to experience, you can get a flavour of what can happen after a referral.

The LA support services

Professionals from these agencies will be able to give you advice on a number of things such as the following.

- *Teaching techniques and strategies*. You might be shown anything from a kinaesthetic approach, to circle time techniques, to a regulated step-by-step programme, to a loop induction system, to Makaton signing. There's a feast of methods, techniques, approaches and systems available to make both the child's learning and development successful and happy, and your part in this effective and enjoyable.

- *Setting management*. Sometimes we just can't see the wood for the trees, and it can take a fresh pair of eyes to spot something within our setting that could be the cause of holding a child back, or preventing their full inclusion. This could be in terms of the room layout, equipment and resources, timetabling, personnel, teaching approaches, or the child's learning style. You may need to do a bit of tweaking to adapt any of these elements, to ensure the child receives effective support.

- *Curriculum materials*. There can be times when a child isn't motivated or stimulated by the activities on offer, and the support services can advise on materials and activities that are known to work. This doesn't mean you have to spend loads of money on re-equipping your setting. The support services may be able to lend you appropriate materials, or point you in the direction of where you can borrow them, such as a toy library or a centre dedicated to a specific disability.

- *Curriculum development*. You can't be prepared for all eventualities and your curriculum may not be fully geared up for inclusion in terms of specific difficulties or disabilities. Again, the appropriate support service will help you to plan the curriculum to ensure it's appropriate and effective for particular children.

- *Direct teaching or practical support for practitioners, and/or part-time specialist help*. This depends on your LA's policy. Some support service professionals will come to your setting to work with a specific child or group of children; others will come to give you practical support, but won't necessarily work with the child themselves. How often they visit you will depend on their workload and the nature of their involvement.

- *Access to learning support assistance*. Again, this will depend on your LA's arrangements. Some authorities have Learning Support Assistants – LSAs (also known as Teaching Assistants, or TAs) – who are allocated to a specific child or group of children (see below). They will either work with the child(ren) directly, or give support during larger group sessions, depending on the child's needs. Sometimes LSAs are employed by a setting and are part of the staff, to be deployed according to the setting's requirements.

The different support services can usually offer specialised help in the fields of:

- Learning difficulties

- Speech and language/communication difficulties

- Sensory difficulties (visual and/or hearing impairments)

- Physical difficulties

- Behaviour difficulties.

Sometimes there will be a designated Early Years Learning Support Service (EYLSS), also offering specialised help, and/or a Portage scheme. Check what your LA is offering – your Area SENCO will be able to tell you. The LA should have provided you with their services' contact details, but if they haven't, ask the LA's SEN department or, again, your Area SENCO. If your setting is private or non-maintained, it's a good idea to link up with your local state-maintained early years providers to share information, facilities, services and best practice.

The child or educational psychological services

The principal practitioners in these services are educational psychologists (EPs) whose responsibilities will include:

- doing more specialised assessments that focus on identifying an additional need or difficulty

- suggesting problem-solving strategies

- advising about behaviour-management techniques

- evaluating the progress of individual children

- offering information and advice about developing SEN/Inclusion policies

- offering professional development in the area of additional needs

- helping to promote inclusion.

It's important to remember that some parents/carers may become very alarmed at the mention of a psychologist, sometimes confusing the term with 'psychiatrist'. Make sure you handle the situation with sensitivity if the time comes that you need to refer a child to the EP.

Advisers or teachers of information and communication technology (ICT) for children with additional needs

Check whether your LA has such a service – again it's a 'local thing'. There's a vast amount of hardware, software and gadgets available to provide support, learning opportunities and experiences, games and activities to assist the development of a child with additional needs. There are programs designed to support specific difficulties and the ICT support service can advise about what's appropriate for a certain child. You may not need to buy the technology since the services will often lend material to a setting for as long as a child needs it.

Social services

There's sometimes a perception that social services become involved with a family only when it's in trouble, when there's abuse going on, or when a child has to be taken into care. But their brief is much wider, and they can offer advice and support to you and your setting, and the child's parents/carers, about other things including:

- applications for benefits or other welfare assistance

- loan of equipment, resources or facilities

- respite care, holiday breaks or other similar facilities

- applications for building grants if the child's house needs adaptations

- societies or venues offering mutual and/or self-help support

- information on voluntary, charitable or independent bodies working in the field of specific disabilities or difficulties

- Positive Parenting courses, offering support and counselling to those parents/carers who feel they need a bit of help themselves.

Speak to your Area Social Worker and find out what's on offer – you never know when it'll be needed.

Child protection services

It's a sad reflection on our society that we need to have these services. Your setting should have a designated child protection worker, whose job is to immediately contact the relevant authorities when abuse of any kind (physical, emotional and/or sexual, and neglect) is suspected.

Once they're involved with a family, the child protection services will liaise with you closely, to ensure the ongoing support and protection of the child. They may even become part of the team working to support the child's additional needs, so a sharing of information and skills will only be for the child's benefit.

 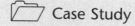 Case Study

Séamus, aged ten months, was born with Down's Syndrome. He had a seizure when he was seven months old, and the paediatrician and health visitor are monitoring the situation, although he hasn't had any more so far. Séamus seems to be going through the usual developmental stages, albeit much later than his peers. The *SureStart* team is working with Judi, Séamus's Mum, who is now a single parent, as his Dad walked out three days after Séamus's birth. The Early Start programme has been put into place, and Séamus and Judi attend the Mums-and-Babies group twice a week, with Baby Music happening in one session and Reading with Babies taking place in the other, as well as the usual interactive games that happen in both sessions. Séamus is clearly benefiting greatly from this social and educational experience, and it also gives the team a wonderful opportunity to observe his development. After being given the contact details of the local Down's Syndrome Association by the *SureStart* team, Judi now meets other parents once a month. She also works on a voluntary basis one afternoon a week in the town's Scope charity shop, while Séamus's granny looks after him.

Medical services

Clearly, it depends on the nature of the child's difficulties whether, and which, medical services are involved. For example, a child with cerebral palsy who also has epilepsy will definitely have medical input, but a child with learning difficulties may have no medical needs at all.

You may find yourself in liaison with:

- health visitors and/or nurses

- paediatric nurses and/or paediatricians (community- or hospital-based)

- child psychiatrists

- general practitioners (GPs)

- physiotherapists

- speech and language therapists

- occupational therapists

- hospital-based counsellors.

If you identify a difficulty that you suspect may be medically-based, you must speak to the child's parents/carers and advise them to take the child to their GP. If a problem is diagnosed, you're likely to be initially liaising with the GP or the child's health visitor.

Learning Support Assistant (LSA) or Teaching Assistant (TA)

This practitioner may also be referred to as the child's support worker, a term that is used more in the early years sector. They're usually allocated to a child or, occasionally, a group of children, to provide appropriate and effective support. Their responsibilities include:

- asking the child's parents/carers about the child's abilities, skills and needs

- planning with the parents/carers, the main practitioner and the SENCO, appropriate and effective IEPs, Effective Learning Objectives, Play Plans or Differentiated Learning Plans (DLPs)

- supporting the child in a variety of situations: one-to-one, small-group, whole-group sessions, with other adults, etc.

- informing the child's parents/carers about the child's progress

- keeping careful records of the child's activities, sessions and learning experiences and their outcomes

- making a contribution to review meetings

- liaising with the main practitioner and the SENCO when preparing the educational advice required by the LA for a Statutory Assessment referral.

You can see that these responsibilities are similar to those of a key worker within a setting, but, as a support worker, they will have a closer involvement with the child who has additional needs.

Private and voluntary organisations

There's a plethora of private and voluntary bodies, usually each for a designated area of disability or difficulty, which offer a valuable source of help and information. They often have information packs targeted at specific readers such as the parents/carers, teachers or other practitioners. You'll find the staff incredibly friendly and helpful, with lots of good, practical ideas for effective support of the child, and the family.

Sometimes the information packs can be downloaded from the internet. Do this, if you can, since it saves postage costs – many of the organisations are charitable bodies, relying on donations to remain in business and they need to keep their expenses to a minimum.

THE CHILD – THE CENTRAL CHARACTER IN THE REFERRAL

The *SEN Code* of Practice recognises that when the child is involved in the planning and implementation of programmes of work or action plans, they're more likely to be successful and have a greater chance of making progress and learning. There are various strategies you can adopt to make sure that the child is at thecentre of the whole process.

- If it's appropriate, speak to them about their difficulties in an ethos of 'We're all special in our own way; we're all good at some things; we all need help with some things.'

- Make sure they understand the targets of their action plan. If they can see where they're going and why, they'll be more motivated to be involved and happier.

- Explain to the child that their parents/carers, you, everybody in the setting and them as well, are a team, working together to help them.

- Watch out for any stress and anxiety that assessment and review procedures may cause the child. Anxiety can develop as a result of simply not knowing or not understanding what's going on. Keep a lookout for any signs of this and talk calmly and positively to the child about it.

- Make sure they understand the role played by outside agents. It might be a bit scary for them when 'outsiders' become involved – again, try to alleviate any anxiety.

- If it's possible, ask the outside agents involved with your setting to visit occasionally, so all the children get used to them. If they can visit at drop-off or collection time so that the parents/carers can establish a relationship with them also, then even better. This helps to reduce the perception of 'them' being 'brought in' if this becomes necessary.

- If a child is being 'looked after' by the local authority and doesn't have natural parents/carers to offer support, establish a positive and cooperative relationship with the carers. It's just as crucial for the 'looked after' child as it is for a child from a more traditional background to see that foster parents/carers or house parents/carers are involved. Let the child know that these adults care for them and are a valued part of the team too.

Note

1 *Special Educational Needs Code of Practice* (DfES, 2001. 10:3).

CD-ROM Resources for this Chapter

Case study JANE (Chapter 7)

Case study ANDREW (Chapter 7)

Case study SÉAMUS (Chapter 7)

Outside Agency Summary Form

Powerpoints

The following presentations are available on the CD-Rom for use in your setting.

The Special Educational Needs (SEN) Code of Practice

The Special Educational Needs Code of Practice

The Special Educational Needs (SEN) Code of Practice provides for

- the inclusion of children in all Early Years provision
- ☐ the involvement of both the child and the parents/carers in all procedures
- ☐ the right of appeal for parents/carers
- ☐ Individual Education Plans (IEPs) that focus only on what is **additional to** and **different from** the rest of the curriculum

The Special Educational Needs Code of Practice

Early Years Action involves

- ☐ identifying areas of concern
- ☐ planning, writing and implementing IEPs
- ☐ holding IEP reviews and planning the way forward

The Special Educational Needs (SEN) Code of Practice

a whistle-stop guide to doing it properly and easily

The Special Educational Needs Code of Practice

IEPs are referred to throughout the *Code of Practice*, and in SEN jargon generally.

At the Early Years stage, you may prefer to speak of *Appropriate Intervention*, or *Appropriate Learning Objectives*.

Photocopiable:

© Collette Drife 2010

The Special Educational Needs Code of Practice

Statutory Assessment involves

- parents/carers, maintained school or nursery school requesting the local authority (LA) to make a Statutory Assessment of the child
- childminders or private nurseries bringing a child to the attention of the LA, which then decides whether a Statutory Assessment is required.

The Special Educational Needs Code of Practice

A Statement of Special Educational Needs

- should take no longer than six months to be issued
- must be reviewed every six months if the child is under five years, or annually above that age.

The Special Educational Needs Code of Practice

Early Years Action Plus involves

- referring to and working with outside agents
- continually monitoring areas of progress and areas of concern
- writing and implementing more specialised IEPs
- holding IEP reviews and planning the way forward

The Special Educational Needs Code of Practice

- The Early Years provider must supply the LA with all relevant records, and information and advice on health-related matters from the appropriate agents.
- When the LA considers an assessment, it asks
  - what difficulties were identified by the provider
  - whether individualised teaching strategies were put in place
  - whether parental views have been considered
  - whether outside advice was obtained regarding the child's

physical health and function   communication skills
self-help skills   perceptual and motor skills
emotional and behavioural development
responses to learning experiences   social skills

The Special Educational Needs Code of Practice

Integration is

placing the child in a mainstream setting and expecting them to change and adapt in order to 'fit in'; integration fails to encourage or facilitate the changes in attitude necessary at institutional and individual levels, to enable the child to participate as fully as possible.

The onus is on the child to change.

The Special Educational Needs Code of Practice

What are the benefits of inclusion?

- Children with additional needs benefit from contact with all their peers and *vice versa*.
- parents/carers become fuller members of the community and are less isolated.
- Positive pre-school experiences mean that parents/carers are more likely to choose mainstream primary schools for their children.

The Special Educational Needs Code of Practice

Inclusion or integration – what's the difference?

The Special Educational Needs Code of Practice

Inclusion is

placing the child in a mainstream setting and ensuring the attitudes, policies and practices at institutional and individual levels enable the child to participate as fully as possible.

The onus is on the setting and everybody involved in it to change, if necessary.

Photocopiable:

© Collette Drifte 2010

Who's who & What's what of SEN

Roles and Responsibilities

Who's who & What's what of SEN

- The *SEN Code of Practice* recognises that time should be allocated to the SENCO for coordination

- The *SEN Code of Practice* suggests that the SENCO should be a member of the senior management team

---

The Special Educational Needs Code of Practice

What are the benefits of inclusion?

- Setting staff and other adults benefit from contact with children who have additional needs.

- Good practice in the care and education of children with additional needs can improve good practice for all the children in the setting.

(Adapted from *All together, How to create inclusive services for disabled children and their families, A practical handbook for early years workers*, Mary Dickins and Judy Denziloe, 2003 [2nd edition] National Children's Bureau)

Who's who & What's what of SEN

The Role of the SENCO is

- to ensure liaison with the child's parents/carers and other professionals who may be involved with the child

- to advise and support other practitioners working in the setting

- to ensure that appropriate Individual Education Plans (IEPs) are being implemented

- to ensure that all relevant background information and records respecting the child are collected, recorded and kept up to date

- to ensure the setting's SEN policy is implemented, monitored & reviewed, and updated when appropriate

---

Photocopiable:

Who's who & What's what of SEN: Early Years Action

The practitioner should

- identify the child's areas of difficulty and of strength
- discuss with the parents/carers the involvement of the SENCO
- provide the SENCO with as much information as possible
- ask the parents/carers about any other problems (e.g. health)
- observe the child

Who's who & What's what of SEN: Early Years Action

The SENCO should

- make sure the parents/carers are completely involved and informed
- collect all known information about the child within the setting
- conduct and/or collect in-house assessments of the child and their progress

Who's who & What's what of SEN

Early Years Action

Who's who & What's what of SEN: Early Years Action

The practitioner should

- maintain accurate and updated records of the child's progress
- liaise with the child's parents/carers, the SENCO and the child to plan an Individual Education Plan (IEP)
- implement the IEP
- be involved in and attend the IEP review

Photocopiable:

Who's who & What's what of SEN

Early Years Action Plus

Who's who & What's what of SEN: Early Years Action

The SENCO should

- decide with the practitioner and parents/carers on the action to be taken, and plan the IEP

- ensure the continual monitoring of the effectiveness of the IEP

- ensure accurate and updated record keeping

- arrange a review meeting (at least once every three months)

Who's who & What's what of SEN: Early Years Action Plus

The practitioner should

- implement the IEP

- maintain regular and careful record-keeping

- if appropriate, involve Learning Support Assistant in planning and record keeping

- be involved in and attend the next review

Who's who & What's what of SEN: Early Years Action Plus

The practitioner should

- collect all the relevant information on the child for the SENCO

- attend a review meeting with the child's parents/carers and the SENCO to decide on the action to take

- plan a new IEP with the external specialist, the parents/carers and the child

Photocopiable:
© Collette Drifte 2010

Who's who & What's what of SEN: Early Years Action Plus

The SENCO should

- work with the specialist agent(s), the child's Early Years practitioners, the child and parents/carers to plan a new IEP, the targets, and the teaching strategies
- ensure the IEP is continually monitored for its effectiveness
- arrange an IEP review at least every three months/once per term, inviting everybody concerned, including the child if possible

Who's who & What's what of SEN: Statutory Assessment

The practitioner should

- collect all the relevant information on the child for the LA
- complete the report (Educational Advice) on the child's progress in response to the LA's request for such advice
- liaise with the external specialist(s), the parents/carers and the child

Who's who & What's what of SEN: Early Years Action Plus

The SENCO should

- request help from the appropriate outside specialist(s)
- inform the child's parents/carers of the LA's Parent Partnership Service
- ensure all relevant records are updated and make them available to the external specialist(s)
- make sure advice and support from external agents are available to both the early years practitioners and the child's parents/carers

Who's who & What's what of SEN

Statutory Assessment & Statements of Special Educational Need

Photocopiable:

© Collette Drifte 2010

Who's who & What's what of SEN: Statutory Assessment

The SENCO should

- collect all the relevant information on the child for the LA including the Educational Advice, and forward it to the LA
- continue to liaise with the relevant outside specialist(s)
- inform the child's parents/carers of the LA's Parent Partnership Service
- ensure all relevant records continue to be monitored and updated

Who's who & What's what of SEN

At all levels – Early Years Action, Early Years Action Plus, and Statutory Assessment & Statements of Special Educational Needs

Who's who & What's what of SEN: Statutory Assessment

The practitioner should

- continue to implement the current IEP
- maintain regular and careful record-keeping
- if appropriate, involve the Learning Support Assistant in planning and record-keeping
- be involved in and attend the Annual or Biannual Reviews

Who's who & What's what of SEN: Statutory Assessment

The SENCO should

- work with the specialist agent(s), the child's EY practitioner, the child and parents/carers to continue the current IEP
- ensure the IEP is continually monitored for its effectiveness
- arrange the Annual or Biannual Review, or ensure the LA arranges it

Photocopiable:
© Collette Drifte 2010

Who's who & What's what of SEN

The Parents/Carers should be encouraged to

- attend all reviews, meetings or discussions regarding their child
- liaise with outside professionals at Early Years Action Plus
- ensure their child has sufficient affection & love, has sufficient sleep, a balanced diet, is appropriately dressed according to the season, and attends the setting regularly

Who's who & What's what of SEN

The Parents/Carers should be encouraged to

- agree to support their child at home through specified activities, targets, programmes etc. agreed with the practitioner
- liaise with the main practitioner and, if appropriate, the SENCO, to plan differentiated programmes of work, IEPs, Play plans etc.
- offer all relevant information about their child that will help in planning effective support
- advise the key practitioner of any problems or difficulties at home that may affect the child's progress (in confidence)

Who's who & What's what of SEN

The child should

- be involved where possible and appropriate in all discussions, plans and arrangements relevant to their support in the setting
- be helped to understand the reason for their IEPs or Play plans
- be helped to understand their programme targets and encouraged to achieve these
- be encouraged to go to their key worker for support, sympathy or any other reason, when they feel the need
- have access to a full, broad and balanced early years curriculum, and be fully included in all activities

Photocopiable:

© Collette Drifte 2010

Helping to Identify Children with Additional Needs

Helping to Identify Children with Additional Needs

- Helping to identify a difficulty must be done in full consultation with the child's parents/carers.
- Names of conditions, syndromes or diseases must never be suggested or discussed without sound evidence; and then used in relation to a specific child only when they have been positively identified and/or diagnosed by the relevant professional.
- Helping to identify a child's additional needs is just that – it is not about unilaterally 'diagnosing' or making judgements.
- Helping to identify means gathering evidence to be shared with everybody, in order to effectively support the child.

Helping to Identify Children with Additional Needs

- When working with a baby, make sure you use the Common Assessment Framework, and/or other checklists that are favoured by your LA and/or setting.
- When working with a baby, always work together with the parents/carers and the other practitioners involved in the baby's care and education.
- Just to reiterate: names of conditions, syndromes or diseases must *never* be suggested or discussed without sound evidence; and then used in relation to a specific child only when they have been positively identified and/or diagnosed by the relevant professional.

Helping to Identify Children with Additional Needs

Helping to Identify Children with Additional Needs

Birth to three years

Photocopiable:
© Collette Drifte 2010

Helping to Identify Children with Additional Needs

Social and emotional development: birth – 3 months

Check whether the baby

- can be comforted by a familiar adult
- responds positively to touch
- interacts best when in an alert state, or in an inactive state
- benefits more from short, frequent interactions or long, infrequent ones
- smiles and shows pleasure in response to social stimulation

Helping to Identify Children with Additional Needs

Social and emotional development: 6–9 months

Check whether the baby

- expresses several clearly differentiated emotions
- can distinguish friends from strangers
- responds actively to language and gestures, and enjoys participating in simple games
- shows displeasure at the loss of a toy or other desired article

Helping to Identify Children with Additional Needs

Social and emotional development: birth – 3 months

Check whether the baby

- sucks their own fingers
- observes their own hands
- looks at the place on the body that is being touched
- begins to realise they are a separate person from others and learns how body parts such as arms and legs, are attached

Helping to Identify Children with Additional Needs

Social and emotional development: 3–6 months

Check whether the baby

- is happy to play peeping games
- pays attention to and responds to their own name
- smiles spontaneously, especially when receiving attention
- laughs aloud, particularly when participating in a game

Photocopiable:

© Collette Drifte 2010

Helping to Identify Children with Additional Needs

Social and emotional development: 1–2 years

Check whether the baby/toddler

- recognises him/herself in the mirror or on photos, and smiles or makes faces at the image

- displays strong feelings for their parents/carers and shows affection for other familiar people

- plays alone and can initiate their own play

- can express negative feelings

Helping to Identify Children with Additional Needs

Social and emotional development: 2–3 years

Check whether the baby/toddler

- is beginning to show an awareness of gender identity

- can indicate their toileting needs

- helps to dress and undress themselves

- is assertive about their preferences and says 'No' to adult requests

Helping to Identify Children with Additional Needs

Social and emotional development: 9 months – 1 year

Check whether the baby

- can self-feed with finger foods

- is able to hold a cup with two hands and drink with assistance

- holds out their arms and legs while being dressed

- can copy simple actions

- shows anxiety when separated from their parent/carer

Helping to Identify Children with Additional Needs

Social and emotional development: 1–2 years

Check whether the baby/toddler

- shows pleasure at new accomplishments, often wanting to repeat the action

- can imitate adult behaviours in play

- shows a sense of self through directing others

- begins to be helpful, such as by assisting in tidying up

Photocopiable:

© Collette Drifte 2010

Helping to Identify Children with Additional Needs

Social and emotional development: 2–3 years

Check whether the baby/toddler

- watches other children and briefly joins in their play
- defends their possessions, sometimes aggressively and/or physically
- begins to play house or other imaginative play
- uses objects symbolically in play
- participates in simple group activities, such as singing, clapping or dancing
- has secure knowledge of gender identity

Helping to Identify Children with Additional Needs

Sensory development (hearing): 0–15 months

(NB Babies' hearing is usually checked at birth using the Newborn Hearing Screening Programme)

Hearing can be affected by

- a family history of hearing problems
- lack of oxygen during a problematic birth
- premature birth
- antenatal exposure to rubella
- some types of birth defects

(cont/d)

Helping to Identify Children with Additional Needs

Social and emotional development: 2–3 years

Check whether the baby/toddler

- is beginning self-evaluation with developing notions of themselves as good, bad, attractive, etc.
- shows awareness of their own feelings and those of others, and can talk about feelings
- displays rapid mood shifts and shows increased fearfulness (for example, of the dark or certain objects such as spiders etc.)
- sometimes displays aggressive behaviour

Helping to Identify Children with Additional Needs

Social and emotional development: 3–4 years

Check whether the child

- can follow a series of simple directions
- is able to complete simple tasks with food without assistance
- washes their hands unassisted and blows their nose when reminded
- shares their toys and possessions, taking turns when directed
- initiates play or joins in play with other children; can make up games
- is beginning imaginative play, acting out complete situations or episodes

Helping to Identify Children with Additional Needs

Sensory development (hearing): 0–15 months

Check whether the baby

- is startled when you clap your hands behind them
- turns towards you or reacts to your voice when you call their name (4–6 months)
- turns their eyes and/or head to locate an interesting sound
- responds to the voice of familiar adults and their parents/carers

Helping to Identify Children with Additional Needs

Sensory development (vision): 0–12 months

Check whether the baby at 0–1 month

- is attracted to faces
- avoids bright lights by closing their eyes
- has eyes that sometimes appear to wander or be turned
- starts to fix on mother's face whilst feeding
- has an intermittent turn in their eyes
- follows large moving objects for a few seconds and begins to show interest in toys

Helping to Identify Children with Additional Needs

Sensory development (hearing): 0–15 months

Hearing can be affected by

- chronic middle-ear inflammation (otitis media)
- frequent ear infections
- temporary hearing loss during an ear infection (also 2–6 weeks afterwards)
- long-term exposure to high-decibel noise, e.g. airports or rock concerts

Helping to Identify Children with Additional Needs

Sensory development (hearing): 0–15 months

Check whether the baby

- makes cooing sounds and other noises (4 months)
- responds to their name and familiar environmental sounds, e.g. the phone or the washing machine (6–10 months)
- points to a familiar object in a picture book when asked (10–15 months)

Helping to Identify Children with Additional Needs

Sensory development (vision): 0–12 months

Check whether the baby at 6–12 months

- has become more skilled in using their eyes to locate and reach objects of interest
- follows objects with their head and eyes in all directions
- is visually alert and curious about their surroundings
- follows an adult's movement across the room
- can recognise familiar people from at least 6 metres (20 feet) away

Helping to Identify Children with Additional Needs

Physical development: 10–18 months

Check whether the baby

- is able to stand and sit down without help
- can carry small objects around
- waves bye-bye and claps their hands
- is beginning to walk without help

Helping to Identify Children with Additional Needs

Sensory development (vision): 0–12 months

Check whether the baby at 2–4 months

- follows a person with their eyes
- has become more interested in toys and objects
- recognise parent's/carer's face and can tell it from other faces
- is able to focus on toys held close to them
- has eyes that are straight and move together in all directions
- is interested in smaller more detailed toys
- reaches for toys, grasps them firmly and examines them

Helping to Identify Children with Additional Needs

Physical development: 0–9 months

Check whether the baby

- drools, mouths and chews on objects
- moves their head when the light is too bright
- is eventually able to hold their head up, roll over and sit without help
- can rise up on arms and knees, and rock
- can crawl (or bottom-shuffle), or hold onto furniture to stand
- is able to grasp objects and move them from one hand to the other

Photocopiable:

© Collette Drifte 2010

Helping to Identify Children with Additional Needs

From 3 years onwards

Communication and Interaction

Watch for the child who

- hardly ever talks or does not talk at all
- stammers or has slow speech, but understands what you say to them, and what they say makes sense
- has delayed or distorted speech that's difficult to understand
- has normal speech but what they say may be odd or inappropriate in context

---

Helping to Identify Children with Additional Needs

Physical development: 18 months – 3 years

Check whether the baby/toddler

- is walking
- can kick and/or throw a ball
- is able to stand on one foot
- can climb stairs, eventually putting one foot on each step
- is able to stand and walk on tiptoes
- can climb over and crawl under objects

Helping to Identify Children with Additional Needs

Communication and Interaction

Photocopiable:

© Collette Drifte 2010

Communication and Interaction

Watch for the child who

- has problems communicating through speech and/or other forms of language
- can't use appropriate verbal and/or non-verbal language
- doesn't react 'normally' in social situations or avoids social situations
- behaves passively and has little or no initiative or curiosity
- seems to be unaware of other people and their needs or emotions
- has unusual voice tone, uses bizarre language and/or ritualistic phrases such as advertisement jingles or slogans

Cognition and learning

Look out for the child who

- has poor scores on assessments or profiles compared with the other children of the same age in their group
- has markedly lower levels of development and play (in all or specific areas) than those of the other children
- finds difficulty in developing their skills, especially in communication and interaction, literacy and numeracy

Communication and Interaction

Watch for the child who

- has normal speech but doesn't seem to understand what you say to them and/or doesn't respond appropriately to other people
- speaks at inappropriate times or makes inappropriate remarks
- laughs very loudly or for too long
- finds it hard to take turns during conversations and / or has poor conversational skills
- has ritualistic or obsessive behaviours or habits

Helping to Identify Children with Additional Needs

Cognition and learning

Behavioural, emotional and social development

Look out for the child who

- is verbally and/or physically aggressive with other children and/or adults
- is introverted or withdrawn, or seems troubled and worried
- is loud and inappropriately outgoing
- behaves inappropriately for their chronological age
- has strange or socially inappropriate behaviour

Behavioural, emotional and social development

Look out for the child who

- has bouts of uncooperative behaviour
- behaves unpredictably and/or has erratic attitudes to learning
- shows little interest in activities and games
- seems to be over-dependent on adults

Cognition and learning

Look out for the child who

- can't deal with abstract ideas and/or generalise concepts from personal experience (older children)
- makes little or no progress in spite of involvement in the nursery curriculum
- doesn't achieve their set targets
- makes little or no progress despite a differentiated curriculum

Behavioural, emotional and social development

Look out for the child who

- does things that may cause self-injury
- can't stay on task, despite support and encouragement from an adult
- regularly disrupts the routine
- doesn't make progress
- is often absent

Photocopiable:

© Collette Drifte 2010

Sensory and/or physical difficulties

See if the child

- has difficulty in coordinating their hands and feet
- experiences problems in balancing
- has poor gross and/or fine motor skills
- moves around clumsily

Sensory and/or physical difficulties

They may have visual difficulties if they

- find difficulty in focusing on an object or have problems in eye-tracking
- have difficulty in doing activities that require visual skills and/or if they have difficulty with hand-eye coordination
- have unusual eye movements such as roving or 'trembling' of the eyeball

Behavioural, emotional and social development

Look out for the child who

- seems to be hyperactive
- can't play with other children, or play with them 'normally'
- can't share or take turns with toys and equipment
- shows poor or no conversational skills

Sensory and / or physical difficulties

They may have visual difficulties if they

- hold books and objects close to their face to look at them
- always sit at the front for stories or television, and then strain to look at the book or TV
- bang into or trip over objects
- have a lack of confidence when moving around the room and/or show anxiety about banging into things

Sensory and/or physical difficulties

They may have hearing difficulties if they

- concentrate intensively on the faces and body-gestures of the adults in the setting
- either don't follow instructions, follow instructions only sometimes and/or follow instructions wrongly
- don't respond to their name, especially if you call them from behind
- watch the other children before doing an action, and then copy the others

Sensory and/or physical difficulties

They may have hearing difficulties if they

- change their voice-tone while they're speaking
- have difficulty doing activities that require listening skills
- have discharges from their ear(s), which don't seem to clear up or which occur quite frequently
- tilt their head when listening to stories, instructions and so on
- appear to be in a world of their own or showing autistic-type behaviours

Sensory and/or physical difficulties

They may have visual difficulties if they

- display abnormal social interaction or autistic-type behaviours
- hold their head in an unusual position
- display eye poking, rocking or other 'blindisms'

Sensory and/or physical difficulties

They may have hearing difficulties if they

- appear to need more visual input and support during activities than the other children in the group
- behave inappropriately or seem to be frustrated without any apparent cause
- don't react to loud or unexpected noises
- shout or talk too loudly without realising it
- have delayed speech or speech that's difficult to understand

Photocopiable:

© Collette Drifte 2010

Planning Effective Intervention and Holding Reviews

Planning Effective Intervention

Appropriate learning objectives are decided on and planned by the

- practitioner
- child's parents/carers
- SENCO
- child, if possible

There isn't a short cut to planning effective intervention – it's a tailor-made, individualised thing! Please don't use Universal Software downloads . . . .

Planning Effective Intervention

- The plan should target the child's difficulties from the point of their strengths.

- Don't overload the child when you choose their targets. Choose only as many as the child can manage – the *SEN Code* says a *maximum* of three or four targets, so choose only as many as the child can manage.

- Choose the targets according to the child's needs and achievement level.

Planning Effective Intervention & Holding Reviews

some practical suggestions

Planning Effective Intervention

The targets should be **SMART**:

Specific – written concisely so everybody knows exactly what the child's aims are.

Measurable – so everybody knows exactly when the aims have been achieved.

Achievable – so everybody knows the targets **can** be reached and **how** the child will do this.

Recorded – so everybody knows the **progress** being made.

Time-defined – so everybody knows by when (i.e. the date) the targets should be achieved.

Photocopiable:

Planning Effective Intervention

- Always select the targets from the point that the child has already reached and has experienced success with.

- Where possible, link them in with the relevant curriculum goals or targets.

- Write the targets concisely, avoiding jargon.

Planning Effective Intervention

- Specify how you'll know when the child has achieved the target. Make the criteria achievable to avoid failure. You can always make the criteria tougher if the child achieves them too easily.

- Decide the 'rewards' to acknowledge and celebrate success. Let the child choose – rewards must be meaningful for them. To avoid creating a distinction between 'work' and 'play', never use a 'play' session as a reward.

Planning Effective Intervention

- Record when the child's performance was checked, by whom and with what result. These details are very important and may be crucial at a later stage.

- Celebrate the child's strengths. This is vital to avoid getting bogged down in what they can't do. There'll be lots of things that they can do, and can do well, so acknowledge these.

Planning Effective Intervention

- Check the targets already achieved – they may need to be taught again or revised. Never move the child on until they've consolidated the earlier skills.

- If a plan is failing the child, try again with new ideas. This is part of professionalism: have the integrity to acknowledge that a plan isn't working, and then change it.

Helping to Identify Children with Additional Needs

Social and emotional development: 9 months – 1 year

Check whether the baby

- can self-feed with finger foods
- is able to hold a cup with two hands and drink with assistance
- holds out their arms and legs while being dressed
- can copy simple actions
- shows anxiety when separated from their parent/carer

Photocopiable:

© Collette Drifte 2010

STANDARDS FOR THE AWARD OF EARLY YEARS PROFESSIONAL STATUS

The award of the Early Years Professional Status requires a practitioner to demonstrate best practice in a total of 39 Standards, organised into six areas:

- knowledge and understanding

- effective practice

- relationships with children

- communicating and working in partnership with families and carers

- teamwork and collaboration

- professional development.

The following are the 39 Standards, and you will see all of them clearly have a direct relevance to practitioners when supporting children with additional needs.

Knowledge and understanding

S1: The principles and content of the Early Years Foundation Stage and how to put them into practice.

S2: The individual and diverse ways in which children develop and learn from birth to the end of the Early Years Foundation Stage and thereafter.

S3: How children's well-being, development, learning and behaviour can be affected by a range of influences and transitions from inside and outside the setting.

S4: The main provisions of national and local statutory and non-statutory frameworks within which children's services work and their implications for early years settings.

S5: The current legal requirements, national policies and guidance on health and safety, safeguarding the well-being of children and their implications for early years settings.

S6: The contribution that other professionals within the setting and beyond can make to children's physical and emotional well-being, development and learning.

Effective practice

S7: Have high expectations of all children and commitment to ensuring they can achieve their full potential.

S8: Establish and sustain a safe, welcoming, purposeful, stimulating and encouraging environment where children feel confident and secure and are able to develop and learn.

S9: Provide balanced and flexible daily and weekly routines that meet children's needs and enable them to develop and learn.

S10: Use close, informed observation and other strategies to monitor children's activity, development and progress systematically and carefully, and use this information to inform, plan and improve practice and provision.

S11: Plan and provide safe and appropriate child-led and adult-initiated experiences, experiences and play opportunities in indoor, outdoor and out-of-setting contexts, which enable the children to develop and learn.

S12: Select, prepare and use a range of resources suitable for children's ages, interests and abilities, taking account of diversity and promoting equality and inclusion.

S13: Make effective personalised provision for the children you work with.

S14: Respond appropriately to children, informed by how children develop and learn and a clear understanding of possible next steps in their development and learning.

S15: Support the development of children's language and communication skills.

S16: Engage in sustained shared thinking with children.

S17: Promote positive behaviour, self-control and independence through using effective behaviour management strategies, and developing children's social, emotional and behavioural skills.

S18: Promote children's rights, equality, inclusion and anti-discriminatory practice in all areas of their practice.

S19: Establish a safe environment and employ practices that promote children's health, safety, and physical, emotional and mental well-being.

S20: Recognise when a child is in danger or at risk of harm and know how to act to protect them.

S21: Assess, record and report on progress in children's development and learning and use this as a basis for differentiating provision.

S22: Give constructive and sensitive feedback to help children understand what they have achieved and think about what they need to do next and, when appropriate, encourage children to think about, evaluate and improve on their own performance.

S23: Identify and support those children whose development, progress or well-being are affected by changes or difficulties in their personal circumstances and know when to refer them to colleagues for specialist support.

S24: Be accountable for the delivery of high-quality provision.

Relationships with children

S25: Establish fair, respectful, trusting, supportive and constructive relationships with children.

S26: Communicate sensitively and effectively with children from birth to the end of the Early Years Foundation Stage.

S27: Listen to children, pay attention to what they say and value and respect their views.

S28: Demonstrate the positive values, attitudes and behaviour expected from the children.

Communicating and working in partnership with families and carers

S29: Recognise and respect the influential and enduring contribution that families and parents/carers can make to children's development, well-being and learning.

S30: Establish fair, respectful, trusting, and constructive relationships with families and parents/carers, and communicate sensitively and effectively with them.

S31: Work in partnership with families and parents/carers, at home and in the setting, to nurture children, to help them develop and to improve outcomes for them.

S32: Provide formal and informal opportunities through which information about children's well-being, development and learning can be shared between the setting and the families and parents/carers.

Teamwork and collaboration

S33: Establish and sustain a culture of collaborative and cooperative working among colleagues.

S34: Ensure that colleagues working with you understand their role and are involved appropriately in helping children to meet planned objectives.

S35: Influence and shape the policies and practices of the setting and share in collective responsibility for their implementation.

S36: Contribute to the work of a multi-professional team and, where appropriate, coordinate and implement agreed programmes and interventions on a day-to-day basis.

Professional development

S37: Develop and use skills in literacy, numeracy and information and communication technology to support your work with children and wider professional activities.

S38: Reflect on and evaluate the impact of practice, modifying approaches where necessary, and take responsibility for identifying and meeting personal professional development needs.

S39: Take a creative and constructively critical approach towards innovation, and adapt practice if benefits and improvements are identified.

List of Abbreviations

BSL	British Sign Language
CAF	Common Assessment Framework
CoP	Code of Practice
DCSF	Department for Children, Schools and Families
DDA	Disability Discrimination Act 1995
DfEE	Department for Education and Employment (title now obsolete)
DfES	Department for Education and Skills (title now obsolete)
DLP	Differentiated Learning Plan
ECM	*Every Child Matters*
EP	Educational Psychologist
EYFS	Early Years Foundation Stage
EYLSS	Early Years Learning Support Service
EYPS	Early Years Professional Status
GP	General Practitioner
HV	Health Visitor
ICT	Information and Communication Technology
IEP	Individual Education Plan
IP	Individual Plan (also known as Play Plan)
INSET	In-service Training
IPSS	Independent Parental Support Service
LA	Local Authority
LSA	Learning Support Assistant
PP	Play Plan (also known as Individual Plan)
PPS	Parental Partnership Service
PSS	Parental Support Service
QCA	Qualifications and Curriculum Authority
SEN	Special Educational Needs
SENCO	Special Educational Needs Coordinator
SSD	Social Services Department
TA	Teaching Assistant

Further Reading

How to Survive and Succeed as a SENCO in the Primary School, Veronica Birkett (LDA, 2000).

Index for Inclusion: Developing play, learning and participation in early years and childcare, T. Booth, M. Ainscow, and D. Kingston (Centre for Studies on Inclusive Education, 2006), available from the Centre for Studies on Inclusive Education, Room 2S203, 5 Block, Frenchay Campus, Coldharbour Lane, Bristol, BS16 1QU. Telephone: 01173 444 007.

Every Child Matters: New Role for SENCOs: A Practical Guide, Rita Cheminais (David Fulton, 2005).

Planning and Organising the SENCO Year: Time-saving Strategies for Effective Practice, Dot Constable (David Fulton Publishers, 2002).

Early Years and the Disability Discrimination Act 1995: What Service Providers Need to Know (Council for Disabled Children, SureStart and the National Children's Bureau, 2003), available from National Children's Bureau, c/o Central Books, 99 Wallis Road, London E9 5LN. Telephone 0845 458 9910; or email ncb@centralbooks.com

Special Educational Needs Code of Practice (DfES, 2001)

SEN Toolkit (DfES, 2001)

All Together: How to create inclusive services for disabled children and their families. A practical handbook for early years workers, M. Dickins and J. Denziloe (National Children's Bureau, 2nd edn, 2003).

Early learning goals for children with special needs, Collette Drifte (David Fulton, 2002).

Encouraging Positive Behaviour in the Early Years: a practical guide, (2nd edition) Collette Drifte (Paul Chapman Publishing, 2008).

A Practical Guide to Pre-school Inclusion, Chris Dukes and Maggie Smith (Paul Chapman Publishing, 2006).

Working with Parents of Children with Special Educational Needs, Chris Dukes and Maggie Smith (Paul Chapman Publishing, 2007).

Recognising and Planning for Special Needs in the Early Years, Chris Dukes and Maggie Smith (Paul Chapman Publishing, 2009).

Right from the Start: Effective planning and assessment in the early years, Vicky Hutchin (Hodder & Stoughton, 1999).

Supporting Inclusion in the Early Years, Caroline A. Jones (Open University Press, 2004).

Taking Part, Hannah Mortimer (QEd Publications, 2000).

Index